Copyright © 2021 All rights reserved worldwide.

No part of this book may be reproduced or transmitted in any form or by any means, electronic or mechanical, including photo- copying, recording or by any information storage and retrieval system, without written permission from the publisher, except for the inclusion of brief quotations in a review.

Warning-Disclaimer: The purpose of this book is to educate and entertain. The author or publisher does not guarantee that anyone following the techniques, suggestions, tips, ideas, or strategies will become successful. The author and publisher shall have neither liability or responsibility to anyone with respect to any loss or damage caused, or alleged to be caused, directly or indirectly by the information contained in this book.

CONTENTS

INTRODUCTION

Imagine your family sitting around a big picnic table, talking and laughing, and enjoying a feast of pulled pork, smoked turkey, twice baked potatoes, grilled fish and chocolate brownies. Now imagine you're not on vacation at a 5-star restaurant, but you're in your own backyard and you've cooked everything on one great appliance.

The Traeger Grill is the one-stop-shop you've been waiting for. Known as the premier wood pellet grill, the Traeger is also of the best smokers and barbeques on the market. It can be used as a smoker, grill and oven, and will quickly become your ultimate favourite appliance.

Barbeque is said to be one of the first methods of cooking – and although the principals of cooking meat over a fire are still the same, the game of barbeque has changed a lot. Traeger entered the scene to take the guesswork out of grilling and smoking, and provide a healthy way for you to enjoy all your favourite meals while using less oil and packing in more flavour.

In this book, we will show you how to not only make your favourite smoked classics – pork shoulder, steaks, fish and vegetables, but we'll also guide you through how to find the best model for you, how to maintain it and how to get the most out of your Traeger. You'll discover how to make a whole smoked turkey, perfect breakfast bacon, cold smoked salmon and yes, even cinnamon buns.

Firstly, we'll tell you all about the art of barbequing, the history of the Traeger and provide you with all kinds of tips on how to make the most of this incredible appliance!

CHAPTER 1 THE BASICS OF TRAEGER GRILL

The History of The Traeger Grill

Joe Traeger invented the first wood pellet grill in Mt. Angel, Oregon, in the early 1980's after becoming increasingly unsatisfied with the grill options on the market. He wasn't a world champion pit master… he was just a regular guy cooking for his family, fed up with the cheap barbeque options that were available to him. The barbeques he was used to had so many flaws. The direct heat directly under the food created 'hot spots' which meant food was often burnt or were left with a chemical taste. He also found that once the barbeque was lit and came up to temperature, there was no way to regulate it. He grew increasingly frustrated and decided he wanted to make something better. The Traeger was born and he never looked back!

By adding wood pellets to the Traeger grill system, he was able to turn his new invention into not only a grill, but a smoker as well. This also eliminated unwanted flames and hot spots, reducing food waste because his dinner was never burnt anymore!

The Traeger Grill has continued to improve since that original version. Often imitated, never duplicated – the original principals of the Traeger still ring true today. Promising to help keep your grilled meats and fish moist and tender, while imparting subtle smoke flavour, the Traeger will deliver! We won't bore you with all the improvements made through a more advanced control system or a state of the art drain system… basically all you need to know is that the current model of the Traeger Grill is as good as it gets on the market. The newest design includes Wi-Fi controls and enables you to see exactly where your grill is hottest to further avoid burning your food. It also includes "Set It And Forget It" features which allow you to monitor your food via an app (WIFIRE technology) so you can add large pieces of meat to your barbeque and let it cook low and slow overnight and wake up to some of the best food you've ever had. We're not saying the Traeger is magic… but it comes pretty darn close!!

We are grateful for all that food that Joe Traeger burned over the years – because without the cheap grills creating hot spots and making him feel fed up, we may not have this amazing appliance today. If you're in the market for a new grill – one that does it all – and you also want to become a master chef in the eyes of your family and friends, the Traeger Grill is right for you.

Now that we've told you about the history of the Traeger, we're going to walk you through what makes the Traeger Grill so special, and why you should be so excited to make it your next home appliance!

Why Are Wood Pellets So Great

For a long time, having a barbeque at home meant you had a stainless steel box connected to either your gas line or a propane tank, that works similar to your oven at home – it heats stainless steel rods via a fire in the bottom and then your food cooks on those rods. This is okay for basic cooking, but it doesn't impart any flavour and makes it incredibly easy to burn your food. It is also true than when cooking this way, you need to add lots of oil to your food to prevent it from sticking, thus making what was a healthy dinner of grilled fish and vegetables, less healthy.

In addition, with a traditional grill, there is very little control over what parts of your grill will get the hottest, and virtually impossible to control flare ups of hot spots caused by fat dripping down from the surface to the fire raging below. Even on the lowest setting, it is possible (and even likely) to dry out lean meats using this traditional grill.

If you're someone who had desired real barbeque flavour from your outdoor cooking experience, you may have switched from this outdated model to a charcoal grill… which is one step better but you will still run into the same problems with hot spots and having very little control over the heat distribution within your grill. A charcoal grill does indeed impart the smoky flavour you are craving if you're a barbeque enthusiast but is fairly high maintenance – they take a long time to heat up and then it is very difficult to maintain the same temperature over the course of a few hours. They take constant attention to keep the embers burning and then you have to deal with ash and dirty coals.

If you're someone who doesn't like to create a massive mess to clean up every time you cook, a charcoal barbeque is definitely not for you. But, you might have considered an electric smoker. These are great for keeping mess to a minimum but the flavour you'll achieve with these machines in nothing compared to the real thing. Most electric smokers on the market reach a maximum temperature of 225F which is not nearly enough heat to penetrate past the surface of a large cut of meat. The flavour can also become artificial or even chemical, which will miss the mark if you're trying to achieve true barbeque flavour.

Barbeque purists may take it one step further than coal and decide to burn their own hardwood in these grills. You'll run into similar problems here with making an absolute mess of your outdoor space, but you will also have to deal with fire hazards! It is very hard to control the level of smoke when using raw hardwood and you may end up with a product that is so smoky, it's inedible. You will have to make sure the wood you are using is completely dry (but not too dry,) and that it's not too green. Basically, it's a lot of guesswork. Even if you do get a great log of hardwood, it is difficult or near impossible to maintain the temperature once you hit it, or to control the rate of burning on the wood. You will end up opening the grill a lot, making the temperature fluctuate even more and wasting valuable time and heat.

When wood pellets entered the scene, everything changed for the home grilling enthusiast! A by-product of sawmills, these wood pellets are made from material that would otherwise go to waste (another reason to love Traeger!) The by-product is ground up finely and then sends into a die that forms it into a small puck. There is no need to use glues or chemicals in the manufacturing process, making wood pellets completely natural and chemical free. This is part of the reason they make food taste so good! The only added ingredient in Traeger wood pellets is a food-grade soybean oil, which is used to help form the ground up wood into a puck shape.

These tiny wood pellets burn just like a real log of hardwood but are much cleaner, more predictable and easier to maintain. You will find a variety of wood pellets at your local hardware store or you can order them in bulk online, but basically once you have your bag, you will just empty it into the hopper on the side of your Traeger Grill and away you go! There is no need to soak, stir or mix. The pellets provided by Traeger come in a variety of flavours which we will outline later, but just know that they are specifically designed to work with Traeger grills. They are developed in American mills and designed specifically for a remarkably consistent burn and result in perfect smoked results, every time! No fuss, no mess, just great authentic wood flavour.

How the Traeger Works

Did you know that the Traeger Grill was equipped with the industry's first brushless motor that automatically adds pellets to the fire, completely eliminating the need for guesswork when it comes to grilling and smoking? This D2 Technology uses a variable speed fan and auger to brush pellets into the fire pot where a hot rob ignites them as needed. Not only does your grill maintain its temperature, but it also circulates flavoured smoke throughout the whole grill which means no more hot spots – nothing will ever burn and the entire cooking surface of your food it surrounded by delicious smoke.

Now, the Traeger Grill takes it one step further with the addition of WIFIRE Technology. That's WIFIRE not WIFI! WIFIRE connects to the Traeger App which allows you to see exactly what is going on in your grill without being anywhere near it or lifting the lid. This way, all the heat and smoke stays inside and you can be enjoying lawn games or a dip in the pool while your dinner cooks, without worrying about overcooking or burning. This is most useful when you're slow cooking something but can be used anytime you use your grill. You can turn your grill on using the app and monitor the doneness of whatever you're cooking. This is great for pre-heating the grill and to take any concerns away about overcooking (or undercooking) your food.

The WIFIRE technology along with the D2 technology allows your grill to reach its desired temperature and maintain it, without you lifting a finger. This makes it incredibly easy to grill, smoke and even bake while imparting added flavour from the wood pellets that make the Traeger Grill so special.

Next up, we're going to walk you through all six of the available Traeger grills. You can't go wrong with any of these models, but allow us to tell you a little more about each model in depth so that you can make the best choice possible to suit your specific needs.

Types of Traeger Grills

There are six different models of Traeger to choose from – all of which have their own features and benefits. Which model you choose depends on your budget and amount of space you have in your yard. No matter which model you choose, you are making the right choice when it comes to Traeger!

Traeger Pro Series

There are two grills in the Pro Series: The Traeger Pro 575 Pellet Grill and the Traeger Pro 780 Pellet Grill. Both are budget and space friendly and come in black or bronze. The only difference between these two models is the actual size of the grill itself, but both offer the same great features including a removable grease tray and heat baffle, a double lined bottom grill, and a pellet chute to remove/change your choice of wood pellets.

Both models in the Pro Series are fuelled by an 18lb pellet hopper on the right side of the grill which you load with whatever pellets you want. If you want to change these pellets for a different flavour later, it is as easy as clicking a button on the side of your grill where there is a pellet chute for easy removal. The Pro Series models also feature a thermometer probe that runs through a port on the right side of the grill. Once the grill is lit, you can close the lid and let it come up to temp and the grill will do the rest of the work! Once you've reached your desired temp (between 165F and 450F,) the D2 technology will release the right amount of pellets to maintain the temperature and perfectly cook your food.

This cookbook will explain exactly what time and temperature you'll need for all your favourite recipes, as well as which wood pellets go best with which food.

Which is best – the Traeger Pro 575 or the 780?

The only difference in these two models is size. Both have removable top racks and feature a grease drip tray underneath the unit. The 575 Pellet Grill is great for small spaces and beginner cooks. It has everything you'll need including space for up to 24 burgers or 4 whole chickens! The 780 is slightly larger and cooks 34 burgers or 6 whole chickens… so really it's up to you what you need and have space for. Both are stunning grills with the same great features.

We recommend the Pro Series for smaller backyards/grilling areas, and for those starting out in the world of grilling and smoking. This unit is great for bachelor pads, small families and for entertaining.

If you're an experienced griller or a professional chef, then we'd recommend upgrading to the Ironwood Series for a number of added benefits which you will see outlined below.

Traeger Ironwood Series

There are two grills available in the Ironwood Series as well – again both based on the actual size of the grill. Both grills offer the same great features as the Pro Series including the same D2 technology that automatically releases your wood pellets once the grill reaches the desired temperature. Both Ironwood Series grills also offer WIFIRE technology that allows you to monitor the inside of your grill via the Traeger App, and they both offer the same removable, easy-to-clean drip tray and heat baffle.

What makes the Ironwood Series grills different is the physical size, as well as the added feature of a 20lb pellet hopper. This model also offers a Super Smoke Mode which allows you to control the temperature and flow of the actual smoke inside your grill as well. This allows you to have a *light* smoke flavour on things like fish or vegetables, or a heavier smoke on things like brisket or pork chops. The smoke ranges from 165F to 225F. When using the higher smoke settings, the Ironwood Series models feature a downdraft exhaust feature that forces air through the rear end of the grill before it exits the grill, which means whatever food you are smoking will be surrounded with smoke flavour for the entire cooking process, not just when the smoke is first burning. This is not only what makes the Traeger so different than other smoker/grills on the market, but also what makes the Ironwood models such a great investment if you're someone who loves smoked food.

Another great feature on the Ironwood Series is the 'Keep Warm' feature. This is especially great for entertaining – when you've spent all day cooking beautiful food, you can keep it just the right temperature without losing moisture or going dry, by using the 'Keep Warm' feature.

Lastly, because the Ironwood Series grills are larger than the Pro Series, there are actually two separate cooking racks which offer more versatility. The top rack is great for lighter smoked items that you want to cook slowly, and the bottom grate can be used as either a grill or can be raised to achieve a light smoke as well. If you're not using the bottom grate and are cooking something on the top rack for a long time, we recommend adding a pan of water to the bottom rack to add even more moisture to whatever you're cooking. This is something you won't find on the Pro Series.

Which is best – the Traeger Ironwood 650 or 885?

Again, the only difference in these two models is size. Both have the feature of two rack spaces allowing you to cook and grill over a variety of surfaces, or add a water pan for added moisture to your slow cooked food. Both feature that 'Keep Warm' setting, which make this the perfect model for more experienced chefs who do a lot of entertaining.

The Ironwood 650 can hold 8 chickens of 5 racks of ribs, so it is definitely a great size for party planning… but the 885 takes it one step further and can hold 10 chickens and even 9 pork roasts.

Both models come in black and will look great on your patio!

If you're interested in the Ironwood Series and want to take your smoking and grilling one step further, there is one more model we'd like to share with you which you can read about below.

Traeger Timberline Series

There are two types of Timberline Series models – both are super grills with all the bells and whistles! They both feature a 24 lb hopper which means you can load your grill with enough wood pellets to smoke everything you want overnight. A full hopper (1 bag of wood pellets) can actually power your grill on low for 20 whole hours. Both models also have an added feature where there is a sensor in the belly of the grill that will warn you if your pellets are getting too low. This has basically made the art of smoking foolproof!

The Timberline Series will reach a maximum temperature of 500F and uses the same D2 technology as every other model. Once your grill reaches the desired set temp, the grill will transport the right amount of pellets onto the rod, slowly releasing smoke into your closed grill, flavouring whatever food you are cooking with subtle, delicious smoke.

What makes the Timberline Series model a super grill is the added feature of an induction fan that basically turns your grill into a convection oven! This feature rolls smoke over your food before exiting the grill's rear vent which means no matter what you're cooking or how many times you lift the lid, your grill will maintain the perfect temperature and will always end up with delicious, moist food. The lid of this model is actually an airtight gasket, along with the double wall stainless steel interior, this grill is basically better than your oven! You will find with the Timberline model, you can use your grill to make anything you can make in your oven including pastries, bread and delicate cakes.

Which is best – the Traeger Timberline 850 or 1300?

The Traeger Timberline 850 is a fantastic grill for luxury homes and anyone looking to add a grill, smoker and convection oven to their outdoor kitchen collection. The 850 model will fit 8 full racks of ribs and includes extra durable stainless steel rods which are fully removable for easy cleaning.

The Timberline 1300 is our most elite model of grill and you won't find a bigger, better model on the market! This is for serious cooks and anyone who loves to entertain. This model includes three racks which combine to provide 1300 square inches of cooking surface. The lowest rack is great for quick high temperature cooking, which we will outline in the rest of this book. The middle rack is great and can fit 12 whole chickens! The upper rack is also removable or can be used for those delicate, slow cooked items. Either way, this grill is going to yield you incredible results, especially when paired with the recipes in this book.

Which grill should I purchase?

As outlined above – any Traeger grill you buy is going to help you create exceptional smoked and grilled food for you and your family or guests. The model you choose will be based on your space and your budget. All the recipes in this book can be cooked on any of the models listed above; however the Timberline model is going to work best for any baked goods or breads, due to the True Convection capabilities. The Pro Series is great for basic grilling and smoking, and the Ironwood will uplift your grilling capabilities from novice or pro chef!

Once you have purchased your Traeger, the first step will be unboxing and assembling your grill. Decide where is the best place for your grill by deciding how far you want to walk from your kitchen area to your serving area. You will also want to make sure your grill is protected from harsh wind areas, and if you have an area that is covered but ventilated, even better! Your grill will last longer if it is protected from the elements – you can purchase our winter cover but placing it out of the elements is also a great idea. You can find lots of videos on how to assemble your grill online, and of course follow the comprehensive user manual that comes with your grill. Now is also a great time to download the Traeger app and connect to WIFIRE. Lastly, you will want to calibrate your pellet sensor and get it set up so you will know exactly when to refill your hopper.

CHAPTER 2 ONCE YOU HAVE RECEIVED THE TRAEGER

Here, we've listed a few things that will make your grilling experience more enjoyable. These are just suggestions of course – once you have your Traeger grill up and running, your entire cooking experience will improve. These suggestions are just icing on the (grilled) cake!

Accessories

The Traeger Grill Brush – While most grill brushes are made of stainless steel, the Traeger grill brush is made of a slab of polished wood, with teeth on the end to get into every nook and cranny of your grill. The reason for this is primarily for safety – although convenience and speed is also a factor. A steel brush may lose pieces of steel which may go into your food if they're not caught, which can be a hazard for your health. With wood, there is no worry.

Along with the grill brush, we also recommend the *Traeger All-Natural Grill Cleaner* which allows you to clean your grill like the pros, without the chemicals.

Extra Racks – These are a great idea if you decide to add extra vegetables or smaller items to your grill. Narrow grill racks make it easy to grill things like asparagus, shrimp and anything that is small that you don't want to skewer. We've provided heaps of recipes for this, but having the extra thin rack will make this easier.

Burger Irons – The hardest part of making great burgers is the fact that they shrink a lot when cooking. With the Traeger Burger Iron, you can flatten your burger patty part way through the cooking process making for the prefect size burger for your bun. This also makes the cooking process faster when it is thin and even, ensuring your burgers are never, ever dry.

Grilling Tongs, Shears, Flipper and Basting Brush – These tools are all optional of course, but they will make your grilling experience more fun… and will make you feel like a real pro! Since Traeger makes everything of such great quality, if you're going to purchase any of these tools, we recommend getting them from Traeger.com!

Instructions

Seasoning

Seasoning is an important first step of grill ownership. This will ensure that your grill is in the perfect state for grilling, smoking, roasting or baking. Seasoning helps lock in the non-stick coating meaning you can use less oil when cooking, and it also makes cleaning your grill easier. This is an important step that takes about 1 hour and should not be skipped.

To season your grill, follow these steps the *first time* you use your Traeger:

Step 1 – Add wood pellets of your choice to the auger at the side of your grill

Step 2 – Plug in the grill and turn the main power switch to "On"

Step 3 – Turn the dial to "Select Auger" and choose "Prime Auger." The pellets will now fall into the fire pot. Once they have all left the Auger and into the fire pot, select "Done"

Step 4 – Turn the dial to 350F and press the dial in to activate

Step 5 – Press "Ignite" and close the lid of your grill. Wait and allow the temperature to come up to 350F. Let it run at 350F for 20 minutes.

Step 6 – Next, raise the temperature dial to 450F and let it run for an additional 30 minutes.

Step 7 – Shut down your grill. This varies by model but will be clear in the user manual for your model. Once the shutdown of your grill is complete, your grill is fully seasoned and ready to go!

Starting Up Your Grill

There are two main options for using your Traeger Grill – it is important to know the difference as it will affect the end product and your cooking experience as a whole. If you do not follow these steps, your cooking experience may result in temperature fluctuations, flames and other issues.

Both methods result in delicious, moist food that will be subtly flavoured with the smoke flavour of your choice. You can refer to the Traeger website if you are unsure of which process is best for you.

The Closed Lid Start-Up Process

This method is super simple! When you've found a recipe you want to cook, simply turn on your grill and select your desired temperature. Let the grill preheat while keeping the lid completely closed for about 15 minutes. This will allow smoke to build in the grill. During this time is a great time to get your ingredients ready – this includes patting meat dry, seasoning vegetables or draining marinade from whatever you are cooking.

The Open Lid Start-Up Process

With this method, you will turn on your grill with the lid open. Wait for about 5 minutes and let the fire start before setting the smoke setting. Next, you'll close the lid and set the temperature waiting for 15 minutes or so for it to come up to temperature. Once you add your food to the grill, you will close the grill and them allow for smoke to build up inside.

A Note About Preheating

Preheating your Traeger grill will take some time, especially with the Timberline models which are larger and therefore take longer to preheat. This is of the same importance as preheating your oven when you are baking bread, so it's a step that should not be skipped. Make sure you leave extra time when planning your meal, to allow your grill to come up to temperature (usually 15-20 minutes.) You can use this cookbook as a guide for how long the cooking process will take, but make sure you account for the preheating time!

Shut Down Your Grill

This grill will take longer to fully shutdown that your average barbeque, because they wood pellets have to burn out and because of the double lined walls of the grill, it maintains its heat for quite a long time. Each model is equipped with a special timer, so you will know exactly how long it will take for your grill to completely shut down. This is important not only for safety, but also so you know when you can add the recommended cover to your grill (when it's cooled completely.)

Cleaning

Because you are not dealing with charcoal or hardwood soot or embers, cleaning your Traeger is incredibly easy. Just like any barbeque, you can simply brush the racks of your grill with a brush or grill brick after each use. Traeger takes it one step further by making all the racks removable, so you could also opt to soak them in hot, soapy water to give them a deep clean. One of the best features of the Traeger Grill is that all the racks come out, which makes it super easy to clean the whole interior – a shop vac will do the trick in a jiffy!

The removable, sloped drip tray included on every Traeger model means that any grease will be collected, which will save on cleaning. You can simple remove this tray and empty it into the garbage or garden, and start fresh each time you cook. (You can also purchase removable drip tray liners direct from Traeger which mitigate some of the messiness of cleaning your drip tray!) With the Timberline model of grill, the remnants in the grease tray are actually heated gently and the vapours mix with the smoke, further flavouring and moistening whatever it is that you're cooking.

Traeger also offers a wooden grill brush in their accessory shop that makes every day cleaning of your grill easy and safe.

Basically, your Traeger is an investment. Just like you love your car, you will love your grill, and you will want to keep it clean and give it some extra TLC every once in a while. We recommend deep cleaning your Traeger once a year (spring cleaning time!) and covering it when not in use to protect from the elements. This will help you keep your Traeger in tip top condition for years!

Make the Most of Traeger Grill

Know Your Wood

There are many different types of wood pellets to air with your Traeger grill. We recommend purchasing Traeger brand pellets for your grill. These pellets were designed specifically for your grill and will yield the absolute best results!

Once you have your wood pellets, it really is as easy as pouring them into the auger on the side of your grill and letting them do the rest of the work!

Flavours of wood pellets range, and this cookbook can help you decide which flavour is best for you, but as a general rule of thumb, apple, cherry and maple chips are milder in smoke flavour and add a hint of sweetness and earthy tones to your recipes. Other mild wood flavours include: alder, apricot, chestnut, mulberry, nectarine, pear and plum. For a more medium flavoured smoke we recommend almond, lemon, oak, orange or peach. Each of these pellets will add nutty or even citrus notes to your food and burn a little more heavily than the milder flavours mentioned above. Lastly, for a robust smoke, you'll want to select a hickory, mesquite or walnut wood.

Traeger also offers a variety of mixed pellets which offer a stunning harmony of flavour! *Traeger's Signature Blend* is of course our favourite – it's a mixture of cherry, hickory and maple… which is a truly amazing blend for all classic barbequed foods. Another great blend is the *Oak and Alder* – this one is particularly great for subtle flavours like seafood and desserts. There's also *A Kiss of Summer* which has a hint of lemon zest and is made from alder and maple – it's said to go great with lobster tails! If you're looking for something bolder, try *Bold To The Bone* for pork or brisket. For the wine lover in your family, there's a special *Winemaker's Blend* that imparts a sweet and spicy aromatic to vegetables or meats. And lastly, there's a *Cherry Mesquite* which is great for smoked desserts because of the sweetness it adds to the grill!

No matter what wood pellets you buy, we recommend storing them in their original, sealed bags. You want to keep these pellets in a dry place and out of direct sunlight which can dry them out and make them burn more quickly than desired. In a dark, dry place and in a sealed bag, your pellets will last indefinitely. You can do your own experimenting with what wood flavours work best for you. We've outlined what we have found works best in these recipes, and please note if you do decided to choose a different wood, it could change the outcome of the recipe… or maybe you'll create something magical! Just be aware of what wood you're using and use the rules of thumb provided in this recipe book as your guide.

Know Your Meat

This book includes a variety of recipes to cook everything from whole poultry to chicken breasts and thighs, to all varieties of pork, different types of steaks and whole racks of ribs, to more delicate cuts like rack of lamb… the options really are endless for your Traeger grill. You can of course also grill the basic items you're used to throwing on the barbeque including burgers and sausages. You can also cook fish and seafood, your favourite vegetables and even bread or baked goods on this awesome, versatile appliance.

The outside of your recipe will start with the quality of the ingredients you choose, so starting with a butcher shop or grocer you trust is a great place to begin! Look for good marbling in your steaks, pork and chicken that is a light pink colour and firm texture. Make sure the fish or seafood you purchase is as fresh as possible or cook it from frozen. Remember that the larger the cut of meat, the longer you will need to cook it. Fast provides deeper flavour in your meat, but you can also cook very lean cuts of meat on your Traeger with great success. It is important to remember that leaner cuts of meat tend to need less time cooking, as they will dry out more easily without the fat content – this is why fattier, larger cuts of meat can be left on the grill longer and cook more slowly.

If you're unsure of what type of meat to buy, we recommend talking to your butcher as they will love to help! Using this cookbook as a guide is a great way to make the most of your cooking experience!

Your Traeger grill has many features to help cook meat as successfully as possible, but just like everything in life it takes a little TLC to be successful. While Traeger does offer the "Set It And Forget It" feature and the convenient WIFIRE app to help make sure your food is never overcooked, if you stray too far from these guidelines or the recipes in this book, you could end up with dried out or overcooked meat. By following the recipes in this book and by reading up on your Traeger before you start cooking, you will reduce the chances of overcooking or undercooking your food on your new grill!

Again – that rule of thumb is: Fat Equals Flavour – look for good marbling in your meats and if you're choosing a very lean meat or fish, it is best to cook on higher heat for less time. If you've got a large cut of meat with lots of fat, you can use the lower cooking settings and 'Set It And Forget It.'

Flavouring Your Food

Everyone knows how delicious a dry rub is on a rack of ribs, or how great a sweet and salty marinade can be on chicken thighs. Cooking with your Traeger grill is no different! The only difference is that you can cook without herbs and spices or marinades if you're looking for a straight smoke flavour, but this book does provide a number of recipes for delicious marinades and spice blends.

You really can't go wrong with dry spices – just buy them from a reputable grocer to make sure you're getting freshest option out there. If you aren't getting huge flavour from your dried spices, you can heat them up gently in a pan before adding them to your meat to help release some of the oils that create flavour.

When using herbs, fresh is also best! Look for vibrant, fresh looking herbs that have great flavour by simply rubbing the leaves together. These can be added at the beginning, middle or end of cooking – just follow the recipes outlined in this book for the best advice.

Grill Set Up

Okay, so you've got your grill set up and seasoned. You've got your recipe ready to go and your wood pellets loaded. Now it's time to get cooking!

Traeger offers a number of great accessories to make this easier including tongs, oven mitts, pans and extra racks. The most important thing to know though is the placement of your ingredients for maximum quality and ease of cooking. You may be used to shifting meat around on your grill top, finding hot spots and 'cold zones'… but with your Traeger, you no longer have to worry about that! In fact, it works a lot better if you set the meat on the grill, close the lid and walk away for the cooking process. This book will provide great tips on how to cook the best chicken, steak and pork chop, as well as how to make the most of vegetables, fish and seafood. No matter what you are cooking, with the Traeger Grill, you are working with pre-set levels of heat and smoke, taking out any guesswork with your grilling experience. Simply place your ingredients in the center of the grill and work outwards from the center – the more delicate ingredients can fan out closer to the outsides. The only decision you'll need to make is if you have the

Ironwood or Timberline, and you'll need to pick which rack to cook on. Again, this book will provide solid advice and instruction on this for easy cooking and awesome results every time!

The Final Ingredient–Temperature

Your Traeger is a master at maintaining temperature, and this cookbook will help you decide exactly which temperature is best based on what you are cooking and what the desired results are.

Understanding how temperature affects food is the best way to achieve the best results. Low temperatures are used for larger cuts of meat with lots of fat – the low heat slowly breaks down the collagen and fat in the meat making it flavourful, tender and moist. This is especially great for things like brisket, pork roasts and pulled meats. For leaner cuts of meat like chicken, fish or lamb, a long, slow cooking process will effectively turn your meat into jerky! A good way to prevent drying out is to use the recipes and guidelines in this book, and to do some research before you start cooking. Also, using a water pan with the Ironwood and Timberline models is another great way to impart an added layer of moisture to the process.

Using the lower rack of the grill and high heat for a short period of time is a great way to grill lean meats like chicken, turkey, burgers or fish. They will still achieve a smoky flavour because of the circulatory nature of the Traeger so not to worry! You can also turn off the smoking feature and set your grill to a set temperature and use it as effectively as an oven when making things like pastries or breads. We've included some recipes for these items near the end of this book and invite you to try them!

Cold Smoking VS. Hot Smoking

Cold smoking differs from regular or hot smoking because the food you're cooking is imparted with smoke flavour but isn't fully cooked in the process. This is achieved by keeping the temperature in the smoking chamber at a low temperature (68F – 85F) and cooked for a long, long time. Generally, something that is cold smoked is cured first, to reduce the risk of spoilage during the cold smoking process. This is a popular way to smoke fish (cured first and then smoked, or just cold smoked) to maintain moisture and flavour of the fish. This can also be used to smoke cheese and other dairy products including yogurt, and for vegetables that you want to leave crunchy. Cold smoking is also the preferred method for smoking liquids such as alcohol for cocktails… but why stop there? Why not try cold smoking juice or coffee?! (We've provided a few smoked drink recipes to help get you started!)

Cold smoking is made possible with the Traeger using a few helpful tips! You can add a tray of ice to the bottom rack of your Ironwood or Timberline model, and keep replenishing it to maintain moisture and a cool temperate throughout the process, but you can also just set the temperature to low and place your cured ingredients in the middle of the grill.

With hot smoking, the temperature is set higher so that the food cooks while it is smoking. This is great for larger cuts of meat, especially when the smoker is set between 225-275. Most of the recipes in this book use the method of hot smoking, but we have provided some tips and recipes for cold smoking as well.

Smoke-Roasting

When you use your Traeger grill at higher temperatures, you will reach a process that is actually known as Smoke Roasting. This is similar to searing in that you get a browned exterior on the outside of your meat or vegetables, but unlike with stovetop cooking or traditional barbequing, you will also achieve a smoky flavour. This is the principal reason Joe Traeger invented the Traeger grill and we think you will find that smoke roasting offers the best of all worlds when it comes to flavouring your food!

With the Traeger grill, you can also *reverse sear* your food. This is a relatively new concept which we've outlined thoroughly in the steak chapter of this book. Reverse searing is when you slow cook your food first and allow it to fully cook and then crank up the temperature and allow it to sear. This sealed in flavours and juices and allows you to achieve perfect doneness and a delicious, crusty, caramelized sear on whatever you're cooking. Cue the drool!

In conclusion, temperature is very important to the smoking process! Follow the guidelines laid out in this book and remember the basic temperature settings:

65-85F is for cold smoking

Up to 275F is for regular smoking

275F and higher is for searing a.k.a Smoke Roasting

Smoking Tips

This book will provide loads of tips for you to add plenty of smoked food to your diet. The main thing to remember is that the smoke flavour should be *subtle*. The Traeger makes this incredibly easy, by adding just the right amount of wood pellets to the heating elements, and the fact that the air is constantly circulating makes it foolproof.

We recommend smoking fish on the top rack of your Traeger at a lower temperature. The flesh of fish is delicate and lean, but unlike leaner meats (where higher temperatures are recommended for a shorter period of time) with fish we recommend a lower heat. Salmon and trout work great as they have higher fat content, but with white fish or seafood, you will want to make sure you are using gentle heat for a medium length of time.

With very high fat items such as bacon, we recommend using a cold smoke for a longer period of time. With a hot smoke on these items, too much of the fat will melt away causing shrinkage and a dry product. Although you can use hot smoke for things like pork belly, we've provided recipes using cold smoke for these high far items.

The more you cook with your smoker, the more experienced you will become and the more comfortable you will be when it comes to knowing the temperatures and timing of your favourite foods. In the meantime, we've provided loads of recipes and tips in this book!

Grilling Tips

In this book you will find a plethora of recipes for all your favourite grilled recipes including burgers, sausages, hot dogs, steaks, pork chops, chicken breast and more. You'll also find recipes for vegetables, tofu, seafood, fish and even baked goods. Anything you can make on your stovetop or in the oven, you can make on your Traeger, so we've added all kinds of different recipes including grilled pizza and even fruit! No matter what you're grilling, you'll find it here.

When you start using your Traeger grill, you will find that grilling is actually a lot easier on this appliance than any grill you've used before. You may be tempted to move your meats around the top of the grill to find the hot spots and cold spots, but once you get rolling with the Traeger, you will begin to discover that this is not necessary.

But utilizing the pro tips we've outlined in this book and by following the recipes as well as caring for your Traeger, you will become a grill master in no time!

Baking Tips

When using the convection features of your Traeger, you will be able to use your oven less and less, and you will want to once you discover how wonderful and easy it is to bake on your Traeger.

We recommend starting with *cold* ingredients when you start baking. This will help to keep pie crusts and cookies crisp on the outside and soft on the inside – to achieve this it's best if your grill is preheated and you add your product to the inside of the "oven" while it is cold. This means if you make a pie for example, you may want to chill it before you cook it. Same goes for cookies, breads and other pastries. We have found that this yields the absolute best results, but feel free to play around with it!

A Note About Winter Grilling

One last note about your Traeger – if you live somewhere that has harsh winters, and you are worried about missing your Traeger during that time, fear no more!!

Unlike most grills that are unable to operate in the winter months, the Traeger is functional even in the harshest winter conditions. This is due to a few reasons. First, the double walled stainless steel body of your grill maintains temperature so well; it also shields the inside of your grill from freezing in the winter. Grilling in the winter is for serious grillers – it takes a little extra work, but imagine this: You clear a path to your grill and brush the snow off the cover. You uncover the grill and preheat it to 350F. This may take a little longer but it will be well worth it! You add a pork shoulder to the grill which you've already dry rubbed and set your timer for 12 hours. The next morning, you wake up and have delicious pulled pork to serve with your cozy winter breakfast of eggs and toast… what a treat!

We've added a few other winter inspired recipes for you folks up north, and we know you'll appreciate them as much as we enjoyed writing them!

Pantry Essentials

Barbeque Sauce – A great barbeque sauce is of the keys to great barbeque food! This is totally up to your own tastes, but definitely look for one that is tangy and slightly sweet… and if you like smoke, look for one with hickory or added smoky flavour. You can use barbeque sauce to baste meat while it's cooking, or serve it afterwards with grilled chicken or pork.

You can find a variety of Traeger brand sauces and marinades online and we also provide some recipes to make your own in this book. Our favourites are the *Traeger Apricot Barbeque Sauce* (goes great with anything smoked using Peach pellets!) *Traeger Sugar Lips Glaze* goes great on chicken or fish.

Rubs - Rubs are a great substitute for a marinade because they don't burn when you are cooking something for a long time. Sometimes the sugar in a marinade will go bitter, but with a rub, you can penetrate the surface of your meat with flavour, without worrying about the burn. Traeger has some great rubs online for everything from prime rib to fish. They've got a great coffee rub and also include things like turkey brine kits. Check it out!

Lemons – Acidity is an important ingredient in most marinades because it helps break down meat proteins therefore making it more tender. Adding a squeeze of lemon to fish or seafood while it is cooking or just before it's done is a great way to add a burst of freshness and flavour.

Salt – Salting meat (especially) is a very important step. Our chefs at Traeger always, ALWAYS have salt on hand for prepping their ingredients, as well as salting during and after the cooking process. With cured foods for cold smoking, you'll want to ease up on the salt as the curing ingredients do contain a lot of salt already. But for large cuts of meat, salting them is very important!

Also adding a dash of salt to meat after its sliced/ready to serve is a great way to wow your guests and act like a real, pro chef!

Oil and Fats – With the Traeger Grill's non stick stainless steel grill racks, you will find you don't need to use much oil at all, but for foods that don't contain a lot of fat like fish or chicken, adding a brushing of good quality oil or spray is a great idea! We like to keep olive oil on hand for drizzling over lean meats and fish after cooking and a good grape seed or canola oil for brushing before we grill.

Explore Your Traeger

Now that you've read up on all things Traeger, you are finally ready to start exploring!

Remember that your Traeger is for more than just smoking and grilling – with the ease of a button (as easy as turning on your oven) you can use this appliance to bake, roast and braise. You can also use it to deep fry, slow cook and steam. Basically, if you can dream it, the Traeger can do it!

Grilling For Every Occasion

In this book, we've provided recipes for every occasion we can think of – to help you be able to spend more time doing the things that matter! From roasted root vegetables at Thanksgiving, to a whole brined turkey… from Hot Toddy's to turkey gravy. From Super bowl Sunday cheese fondue, to loaded baked buffalo chicken dip. From Irish soda bread on St. Patrick's Day to a smoked Margarita on Cinco De Mayo. From short rib chilli to maple bacon doughnuts…

And this cookbook isn't just for special occasions… it also suits every dietary restriction and diet out there! In fact, adding more grilled food to your diet is an excellent, easy way to follow a paleo or keto diet, and it's also great for low-fat diets if you are concerned about added oils to your food. Basically, this book (and this grill!) is for everyone!

The Art Of Barbeque

The art of barbequing goes as far back as cooking does – some might say that barbeque was the first method of cooking – developed by cavemen when they discovered fire! Since then, barbeque has become a staple in many cultures, and loved worldwide. With the invention of the electric smoker and the propane barbeque, it has become accessible for every home to have an affordable, easy-to-use grill in their backyards. Barbeque is now a very important part of American culture and it is said that the founding fathers of America were huge barbeque fans, especially George Washington. Barbeque plays an especially large role in Southern American culture where it is prized for bringing bold flavours, rich sauces and age old techniques. People in the South loved it so much, they began having competitions around who made the best barbequed food which has led to a multibillion dollar industry. "Pit Masters" from all over the world join competitions every summer to show why their smoked and grilled food is the ultimate.

Barbeque food isn't just popular in the Western world though. In Japanese and Korean cultures, grilling is a communal affair with restaurants and homes sporting portable table-top grills for everyone to grill their own meat and fish as they dine. Yakitori restaurants have become so popular they've even arrived in North America! Quick grilling and barbequing is here to stay… and now you can bring it to your own home with the Traeger Grill!

One Last Thing

No matter what way you look at it, barbeque is loved around the world, and now it is going to be enjoyed and mastered in *your* home.

We think the reason barbeque culture has spread so quickly and lasted for so long, is because part of the art of barbeque is the art of *sharing* food. A large piece of smoked meat and a platter of grilled vegetables is the perfect food to serve to just about anyone. A smoked fish alongside some great appetizers, or even something as simple as hamburgers and hot dogs, or a grilled cheese sandwich… Barbeque means family! And this barbeque is going to give you more time with your family with its D2 technology, WIFIRE app and "Set It And Forget It" features. Long gone are the days of you babysitting your grill, waiting patiently for your food to cook while dancing it around the grill looking for the best spot. Long gone are the days of flavourless, bland steaks or overcooked chicken breast. Long gone are the days of missing out on time at your own pool party so that you can carefully watch the shrimp skewers. Everything is made easy with the Traeger grill, and your life is promised to improve!

We hope this book provides you with lots of great ideas! Rain or shine, sunny days or in-for-the-winter, any day is a great day to get out there and grill. Your Traeger can help you live a healthier, simpler lifestyle and help give you some of your time back. And remember, barbeque is about family…. So get out there and cook something great!

Troubleshooting

Your WIFIRE app will have some helpful tips when it comes to troubleshooting your Traeger, and you can also refer to your user manual. There are however a few things that could come up which we will cover here:

What do I do if my Traeger Grill won't start?

First, check to see if your grill is in "Demo" mode. The controller will quickly reboot and should turn on after that. If that is unsuccessful, check to see if the fan is running. DO NOT TOUCH anything inside the grill especially the Hot Rod. Just listen closely to see if the fan is running when you turn the grill on. If it's not, it could be a pellet jam.

What do I do if the pellets are not moving though?

A pellet jam is a common problem with a simple solution. Simply flush the pellets through the auger. You can check to make sure your pellets are in good condition – if they have been in the auger for a long time in the elements, they may have become dry or brittle. They should ideally have a nice sheen to them and have a "snap" if you break one. If this is not the case, we recommend starting with new, fresh wood pellets. This will help reduce the chances of them jamming in the auger.

What do I do if my grill is not maintaining smoke or temperature?

If there is too much smoke coming from your grill, this could be a similar problem with the pellets. Make sure they are fresh, shiny and have a nice break to them. If they are very dry or damp at all, they will smoke a lot and not produce an even temperature.

If there is a build-up of grease in the trap or if it is overflowing, or if you have not cleaned your grill in a long time, there could be blockages around the fan which would result in uneven smoke, or a failure to distribute heat. This is also a simple fix by emptying the grease trap and giving your grill a good, deep clean and making sure the fan is running properly.

What do I do if my grill catches fire?

Of course, with any heating element, there is always the risk of fire and flames. The Traeger grill has many safety ratings because of its specific design, but there could always be things that come up. The most common reason a fire would start is if the grease tray had not been emptied and it came into contact with the flame. This is unlikely, but it is possible, so it's a good idea to make sure you empty and clean the grease tray regularly.

These are the most common problems you might encounter with your Traeger. Most have quick and easy solutions and will be mitigated with proper seasoning and regular cleaning of your grill. For any other problems that arise, please contact your Traeger dealership or customer service through the website immediately.

CHAPTER 3 TOP 10 RECIPES

3-2-1 Grilled BBQ Ribs

Prep time: 15 minutes | Cook time: 6 hours | Serves 6

⅓ cup yellow mustard

½ cup apple juice, divided, plus more as needed

1 tablespoon Worcestershire sauce

2 rack baby back pork ribs, membrane removed

Traeger Pork &Poultry Rub, to taste

½ cup dark brown sugar

⅓ cup honey, warmed

1 cup Traeger 'Que BBQ sauce

1.   Stir together the mustard, ¼ cup of apple juice, and Worcestershire sauce in a small bowl. Spread the mustard mixture thinly on both sides of the ribs and season to taste with Traeger Pork & Poultry Rub.

2.   When ready to cook, set Traeger temperature to 180ºF (82ºC) and preheat, lid closed for 15 minutes. Smoke the ribs for 3 hours, meat-side up.

3.   Once complete, transfer the ribs to a rimmed baking sheet and increase the grill temperature to 225ºF (107ºC).

4.   Tear off four long sheets of heavy-duty aluminum foil. Top with a rack of ribs and pull up the sides to keep the liquid enclosed. Scatter the rack with half the brown sugar, then top with half the honey and half the remaining apple juice. If you want more tender ribs, you can use a bit more apple juice. Lay another piece of foil on top and tightly crimp the edges so there is no leakage. Repeat with the remaining rack of ribs.

5.   Return the foiled ribs to the grill and cook for another 2 hours.

6.   Remove the foil from the ribs and brush the ribs with Traeger 'Que Sauce on both sides. Discard the foil.

7.   Place the ribs directly on the grill and continue to grill for 30 to 60 minutes more, or until the sauce has tightened.

8.   Allow the ribs to cool for 5 to 10 minutes and serve.

Traeger Smoked Pulled Pork

Prep time: 10 minutes | Cook time: 9 hours | Serves 8

1 (6- to 9-pound / 2.7- to 4.1-kg) bone-in pork shoulder, trimmed

Traeger Big Game Rub, as needed

2 cup apple cider

Traeger 'Que BBQ sauce, to taste

1. Season the pork butt generously with Traeger Big Game Rub on all sides and allow to sit for 20 minutes.
2. When ready to cook, set Traeger temperature to 250ºF (121ºC) and preheat, lid closed for 15 minutes.
3. Arrange the pork butt, fat-side up, directly on the grill and cook for about 3 to 5 hours, or until the internal temperature registers 160ºF (71ºC).
4. Remove the pork butt from the grill.
5. Stack 4 large pieces of aluminum foil on top of each other on a large baking sheet, ensuring they are wide enough to wrap the pork butt entirely on all sides. If not, overlap the foil pieces to create a wider base. Put the pork butt in the center on the aluminum foil, then bring up the sides of the foil a little bit before pouring the apple cider on top of the pork butt. Wrap the foil tightly around the pork butt, ensuring the cider does not escape.
6. Return the foil-wrapped pork butt, fat-side up, to the grill and cook for about 3 to 4 hours, or until a meat thermometer inserted in the thickest part of the meat reaches 204ºF (96ºC). The cooking time depends on the size of the pork butt.
7. Remove the pork butt from the grill. Let rest for 45 minutes in the foil packet.
8. Remove the pork from the foil and pour off any excess liquid into a fat separator.
9. Put the pork butt in a large dish and shred the meat, removing and discarding the bone and any excess fat. Add separated liquid back into pork and season with additional Traeger Big Game Rub to taste. Optionally, add Traeger 'Que BBQ Sauce or your favorite BBQ sauce to taste. Serve immediately.

Easy Baked Potatoes

Prep time: 15 minutes | Cook time: 1 hours | Serves 4

6 russet potatoes, scrubbed and dried

3 tablespoons canola oil

1 tablespoon kosher salt

Optional Toppings:

Butter

Sour cream

Bacon bits

Cheddar cheese

Fresh chives

1.   Place the potatoes in a large bowl and coat with the canola oil, then season with salt.

2.   When ready to cook, set Traeger temperature to 450ºF (232ºC) and preheat, lid closed for 15 minutes.

3.   Arrange the potatoes directly on the grill and bake until fork-tender, about 30 to 40 minutes. Serve the potatoes hot with the toppings, if desired.

Traeger Prime Rib Roast

Prep time: 5 minutes | Cook time: 4 hours | Serves 8

1 (5- to 7-bone) prime rib roast

Traeger Prime Rib Rub, as needed

1.   Generously season the roast with the Traeger Prime Rib Rub on all sides and wrap in plastic wrap. Place in the refrigerator for 24 hours.

2.   When ready to cook, set Traeger temperature to 500ºF (260ºC) and preheat, lid closed for 15 minutes.

3.   Put the prime rib, fat-side up, directly on the grill and cook for 30 minutes.

4.   When done, reduce the grill temperature to 300ºF (149ºC). Continue to cook for 3 to 4 hours or until cooked to the desired internal temperature, 120ºF (49ºC) for rare, 130ºF (54ºC) for medium rare, 140ºF (60ºC) for medium or 150ºF (66ºC) for well done. The cooking time depends on the size of your roast and desired finished temperature.

5.   Remove the roast from the grill and cool for 30 minutes before carving.

Beer Can Whole Chicken

5 pounds (2.3 kg) whole chicken

Traeger Chicken Rub, as needed

1 can beer

1.   Tuck the wing tips back and truss the chicken legs together. Generously season the whole chicken, including the cavity, with Traeger Chicken Rub.

2.   Place the chicken onto the open can of beer so that the chicken is sitting upright with the can in its cavity.

3.   When ready to cook, set the Traeger to 350ºF (177ºC) and preheat, lid closed for 15 minutes.

4.   Put the chicken on a sheet tray and place directly on the grill. Cook for 60 to 75 minutes or until a meat thermometer inserted in the thickest part of the breast reaches 165ºF (74ºC).

5.   Remove the chicken from the grill and allow to cool for 5 to 10 minutes before serving.

CHAPTER 4 RUB, SAUCES, AND SEASONING

Homemade Chicken Rub

Prep time: 10 minute | Cook time: 0 minute | Makes 1/4 cup

2 tablespoons packed light brown sugar

1½ teaspoons coarse kosher salt

1¼ teaspoons garlic powder

½ teaspoon onion powder

½ teaspoon freshly ground black pepper

½ teaspoon ground chipotle chile pepper

½ teaspoon smoked paprika

¼ teaspoon dried oregano leaves

¼ teaspoon mustard powder

¼ teaspoon cayenne pepper

1. In a small airtight container or zip-top bag, combine the brown sugar, salt, garlic powder, onion powder, black pepper, chipotle pepper, paprika, oregano, mustard, and cayenne.

2. Close the container and shake to mix. Unused rub will keep in an airtight container for months.

Garlicky Dill Seafood Rub

Prep time: 5 minutes | Cook time: 0 minute | Makes 5 tablespoons

2 tablespoons coarse kosher salt

2 tablespoons dried dill weed

1 tablespoon garlic powder

1½ teaspoons lemon pepper

1. In a small airtight container or zip-top bag, combine the salt, dill, garlic powder, and lemon pepper.

2. Close the container and shake to mix. Unused rub will keep in an airtight container for months.

Classic Cajun Rub

Prep time: 10 minute | Cook time: 0 minute | Makes 3 tablespoons

1 teaspoon freshly ground black pepper

1 teaspoon onion powder

1 teaspoon coarse kosher salt

1 teaspoon garlic powder

1 teaspoon sweet paprika

½ teaspoon cayenne pepper

½ teaspoon red pepper flakes

½ teaspoon dried oregano leaves

½ teaspoon dried thyme

½ teaspoon smoked paprika

1.   In a small airtight container or zip-top bag, combine the black pepper, onion powder, salt, garlic powder, sweet paprika, cayenne, red pepper flakes, oregano, thyme, and smoked paprika.

2.   Close the container and shake to mix. Unused rub will keep in an airtight container for months.

Simple Espresso Brisket Rub

Prep time: 10 minute | Cook time: 0 minute | Makes ½ cup

3 tablespoons coarse kosher salt

2 tablespoons ground espresso coffee

2 tablespoons freshly ground black pepper

1 tablespoon garlic powder

1 tablespoon light brown sugar

1½ teaspoons dried minced onion

1 teaspoon ground cumin

1.   In a small airtight container or zip-top bag, combine the salt, espresso, black pepper, garlic powder, brown sugar, minced onion, and cumin.

2.   Close the container and shake to mix. Unused rub will keep in an airtight container for months.

Brown Sugar Rub

Prep time: 10 minute | Cook time: 0 minute | Makes ¼ cup

2 tablespoons light brown sugar

1 teaspoon coarse kosher salt

1 teaspoon garlic powder

1 teaspoon onion powder

1 teaspoon sweet paprika

½ teaspoon freshly ground black pepper

½ teaspoon cayenne pepper

½ teaspoon dried oregano leaves

¼ teaspoon smoked paprika

1.   In a small airtight container or zip-top bag, combine the brown sugar, salt, garlic powder, onion powder, sweet paprika, black pepper, cayenne, oregano, and smoked paprika.

2.   Close the container and shake to mix. Unused rub will keep in an airtight container for months.

Easy All-Purpose Dry Rub

Prep time: 10 minute | Cook time: 0 minute | Makes 2 and ½ cups

½ cup paprika, or ⅓ cup smoked paprika

¼ cup kosher salt

¼ cup freshly ground black pepper

¼ cup brown sugar

¼ cup chile powder

3 tablespoons ground cumin

2 tablespoons ground coriander

1 tablespoon cayenne pepper, or to taste

1.   Combine all ingredients in a bowl and mix well with a fork to break up the sugar and combine the spices. Mixture will keep in an airtight container, out of the light, for a few months.

California Beef Rub

Prep time: 10 minute | Cook time: 0 minute | Makes ⅓ cups

2 tablespoons finely ground coffee

1½ tablespoons kosher salt

1½ tablespoons granulated garlic

1 heaping teaspoon black pepper

1 tablespoon brown sugar

¼ teaspoon cayenne pepper

¼ teaspoon ground cloves

¼ teaspoon cinnamon

1.   Combine all ingredients in a bowl and mix well with a fork to break up the sugar and combine the spices. Mixture will keep in an airtight container, out of the light, for a few months.

Sweet-Spicy Cinnamon Rub

Prep time: 10 minute | Cook time: 0 minute | Makes ¼ cups

2 tablespoons light brown sugar

1 teaspoon coarse kosher salt

1 teaspoon garlic powder

1 teaspoon onion powder

1 teaspoon sweet paprika

½ teaspoon freshly ground black pepper

½ teaspoon cayenne pepper

½ teaspoon dried oregano leaves

½ teaspoon ground ginger

½ teaspoon ground cumin

¼ teaspoon smoked paprika

¼ teaspoon ground cinnamon

¼ teaspoon ground coriander

¼ teaspoon chili powder

1.   In a small airtight container or zip-top bag, combine the brown sugar, salt, garlic powder, onion powder, sweet paprika, black pepper, cayenne, oregano, ginger, cumin, smoked paprika, cinnamon, coriander, and chili powder.

2.   Close the container and shake to mix. Unused rub will keep in an airtight container for months.

Spicy Coffee Rub

Prep time: 5 minutes | Cook time: 0 minute | Makes 1 cups

¼ cup finely ground dark-roast coffee

¼ cup ancho chile powder

¼ cup dark brown sugar, tightly packed

2 tablespoons smoked paprika

2 tablespoons kosher salt

1 tablespoon ground cumin

1.   In a small bowl, mix all the ingredients thoroughly, massaging the mixture with your fingers to break down the dark brown sugar into fine crystals.

2.   Liberally sprinkle a thin layer of the rub onto the steak, then pat it in with your fingers so it adheres.

Fast Cumin Salt

Prep time: 5 minutes | Cook time: 0 minute | Makes ¼ cups

1 teaspoon cumin seeds

¼ cup medium-coarse or flaky sea salt

Pinch red pepper flakes (optional)

Pinch cayenne or hot paprika (optional)

1.   Toast cumin seeds in a dry skillet over medium-high heat until fragrant and lightly colored, about 1 minute.

2.   Grind very coarsely in a mortar or spice mill.

3.   Combine in a bowl with salt and stir together.

4.   Add red pepper flakes or cayenne, if using.

Burger Seasoning

Prep time: 10 minute | Cook time: 0 minute | Makes 2 tablespoons

1 teaspoon coarse kosher salt

1 teaspoon garlic powder

1 teaspoon dried minced onion

1 teaspoon onion powder

½ teaspoon sweet paprika

¼ teaspoon mustard powder

¼ teaspoon celery seed

1 teaspoon freshly ground black pepper

1.   In a small airtight container or zip-top bag, combine the salt, garlic powder, minced onion, onion powder, black pepper, sweet paprika, mustard powder, and celery seed.

2.   Close the container and shake to mix. Unused burger shake will keep in an airtight container for months.

Simple Jerk Seasoning

Prep time: 10 minute | Cook time: 0 minute | Makes ¼ cup

1 tablespoon allspice berries

¼ teaspoon nutmeg pieces (crack a whole nutmeg with a hammer)

1 teaspoon black peppercorns

2 teaspoons dried thyme

1 teaspoon cayenne, or to taste

1 tablespoon paprika

1 tablespoon sugar

1 tablespoon salt

2 teaspoons minced garlic

2 teaspoons minced ginger (or 2 teaspoons ground ginger)

1.   Put allspice, nutmeg, peppercorns and thyme in a spice or coffee grinder and grind to a fine powder.

2.   Mix in remaining ingredients and use immediately. To use later, omit garlic and ginger and store in a tightly covered container; add garlic and ginger immediately before using.

Rosemary Lamb Seasoning

Prep time: 5 minutes | Cook time: 0 minute | Makes 2 tablespoons

2 teaspoons dried rosemary leaves

2 teaspoons coarse kosher salt

1 teaspoon garlic powder

1 teaspoon freshly ground black pepper

½ teaspoon onion powder

½ teaspoon dried minced onion

1.   In a small airtight container or zip-top bag, combine the rosemary, salt, garlic powder, black pepper, onion powder, and minced onion.

2.   Close the container and shake to mix. Unused seasoning will keep in an airtight container for months.

Classic Tea Injectable

Prep time: 10 minute | Cook time: 0 minute | Makes 2 cups

¼ cup favorite spice rub or shake

2 cups water

1.   Place the rub in a standard paper coffee filter and tie it up with kitchen string to seal.

2.   In a small pot over high heat, bring the water to a boil.

3.   Drop the filter into the boiling water and remove the pot from the heat. Let it steep for 30 minute.

4.   Remove and discard the filter. Discard any unused tea after injecting the meat.

Buttered Garlicky Injectable

Prep time: 5 minutes | Cook time: 0 minute | Makes 2 cups

16 tablespoons (2 sticks) salted butter

2 tablespoons salt

1½ tablespoons garlic powder

1.   Use this injectable quickly and clean up with hot water. Because butter solidifies so quickly, it can easily clog your injector.

Herbed Compound Butter

Prep time: 10 minute | Cook time: 0 minute | Makes ½ cup

8 tablespoons unsalted butter

1 tablespoon herb leaves, minced

1 small shallot, peeled and minced

2 teaspoons freshly squeezed lemon or lime juice

Splash Champagne or white-wine vinegar

1.   Put the butter on a cutting board and, using a fork, cut the other ingredients into it until the butter is creamy and smooth. Scrape the butter together with a chef's knife, and form it into a rough log. If making ahead of time, roll it tightly in a sheet of plastic wrap and refrigerate or freeze until ready to use.

Homemade Lobster Butter

Prep time: 5 minutes | Cook time: 40 minute | Makes ½ cup

Shells of cooked lobsters, crushed into small pieces

8 tablespoons (1 stick) unsalted butter per lobster

1.   Heat grill to 300ºF (149ºC). Put lobster shells on the largest sheet pan you can fit in the oven, and allow them to dry and roast, about 15 to 20 minute. Remove and set aside.

2.   Meanwhile, melt 1 stick butter per lobster in a large bowl or double boiler set over simmering water, making sure bowl does not touch the surface of water. Add lobster shells to the melted butter and simmer gently, without boiling, for about 20 minute.

3.   Strain the melted butter through a cheesecloth-lined sieve into another bowl, then set that bowl into ice to chill. Cover bowl and refrigerate to set, then skim off the top and discard any liquids. Use within a few days, or freeze for up to a few weeks.

Teriyaki Marinade

Prep time: 5 minutes | Cook time: 0 minute | Makes 1 cup

¼ cup water

¼ cup soy sauce

¼ cup packed light brown sugar

¼cup Worcestershire sauce

2 garlic cloves, sliced

1.   In a small bowl, whisk the water, soy sauce, brown sugar, Worcestershire sauce, and garlic until combined. Refrigerate any unused marinade in an airtight container for 2 or 3 days.

Classic Italian Marinade

1 cup extra-virgin olive oil

¾ cup red wine vinegar

Zest of 1 lemon

¼ cup freshly squeezed lemon juice (about 2 lemons)

4 cloves garlic, peeled, smashed and roughly chopped

1 bay leaf

1 tablespoon thyme leaves

1 tablespoon oregano leaves

1 tablespoon basil leaves, rolled and chopped into chiffonade

1 teaspoon granulated sugar

1 teaspoon kosher salt

1 teaspoon freshly cracked black pepper

1 teaspoon red pepper flakes, or to taste

1.   Whisk together all the ingredients in a large bowl. Refrigerate any unused marinade in an airtight container for 2 or 3 days.

CHAPTER 5 MEATS

Classic Texas Smoked Brisket

Prep time: 15 minutes | Cook time: 16 to 20 hours | Serves 12 to 15

1 (12-pound / 340-g) full packer brisket

2 tablespoons yellow mustard

1 batch espresso brisket rub

Worcestershire mop and spritz, for spritzing

1. Supply your Traeger with wood pellets and follow the start-up procedure. Preheat the grill, with the lid closed, to 225ºF (107ºC).

2. Using a boning knife, carefully remove all but about ½ inch of the large layer of fat covering one side of your brisket.

3. Coat the brisket all over with mustard and season it with the rub. Using your hands, work the rub into the meat. Pour the mop into a spray bottle.

4. Place the brisket directly on the grill grate and smoke until its internal temperature reaches 195°F (91ºC), spritzing it every hour with the mop.

5. Pull the brisket from the grill and wrap it completely in aluminum foil or butcher paper. Place the wrapped brisket in a cooler, cover the cooler, and let it rest for 1 or 2 hours.

6. Remove the brisket from the cooler and unwrap it.

7. Separate the brisket point from the flat by cutting along the fat layer and slice the flat. The point can be saved for burnt ends (see Sweet Heat Burnt Ends), or sliced and served as well.

Homemade Mesquite Smoked Brisket

Prep time: 15 minutes | Cook time: 12 to 16 hours | Serves 8 to 12

1 (12-pound / 340-g) full packer brisket

2 tablespoons yellow mustard (you can also use soy sauce)

Salt, to taste

Freshly ground black pepper, to taste

1.   Supply your Traeger with wood pellets and follow the start-up procedure. Preheat the grill, with the lid closed, to 225ºF (107ºC).

2.   Using a boning knife, carefully remove all but about ½ inch of the large layer of fat covering one side of your brisket.

3.   Coat the brisket all over with mustard and season it with salt and pepper.

4.   Place the brisket directly on the grill grate and smoke until its internal temperature reaches 160ºF (71ºC) and the brisket has formed a dark bark.

5.   Pull the brisket from the grill and wrap it completely in aluminum foil or butcher paper.

6.   Increase the grill's temperature to 350ºF (177ºC) and return the wrapped brisket to it. Continue to cook until its internal temperature reaches 190ºF (88ºC).

7.   Transfer the wrapped brisket to a cooler, cover the cooler, and let the brisket rest for 1 or 2 hours.

8.   Remove the brisket from the cooler and unwrap it.

9.   Separate the brisket point from the flat by cutting along the fat layer, and slice the flat. The point can be saved for burnt ends (see Sweet Heat Burnt Ends), or sliced and served as well.

Smoked Burnt Ends

Prep time: 30 minute | Cook time: 6 hours | Serves 8 to 10

1 (6-pound / 170-g) brisket point

2 tablespoons yellow mustard

1 batch sweet brown sugar rub

2 tablespoons honey

1 cup barbecue sauce

2 tablespoons light brown sugar

1.   Supply your Traeger with wood pellets and follow the start-up procedure. Preheat the grill, with the lid closed, to 225ºF (107ºC).

2.   Using a boning knife, carefully remove all but about ½ inch of the large layer of fat covering one side of your brisket point.

3.   Coat the point all over with mustard and season it with the rub. Using your hands, work the rub into the meat.

4.   Place the point directly on the grill grate and smoke until its internal temperature reaches 165ºF (74ºC).

5.   Pull the brisket from the grill and wrap it completely in aluminum foil or butcher paper.

6.   Increase the grill's temperature to 350ºF (177ºC) and return the wrapped brisket to it. Continue to cook until its internal temperature reaches 185ºF (85ºC).

7.   Remove the point from the grill, unwrap it, and cut the meat into 1-inch cubes. Place the cubes in an aluminum pan and stir in the honey, barbecue sauce, and brown sugar.

8.   Place the pan in the grill and smoke the beef cubes for 1 hour more, uncovered. Remove the burnt ends from the grill and serve immediately.

Reverse-Seared Tri-Tip Roast

Prep time: 10 minute | Cook time: 2 to 3 hours | Serves 4

1½ pounds (680 g) Tri-Tip roast

1 batch Espresso Brisket Rub

1.   Supply your Traeger with wood pellets and follow the start-up procedure. Preheat the grill, with the lid closed, to 180ºF (82ºC).

2.   Season the Tri-Tip roast with the rub. Using your hands, work the rub into the meat.

3.   Place the roast directly on the grill grate and smoke until its internal temperature reaches 140°F (60ºC).

4.   Increase the grill's temperature to 450°F and continue to cook until the roast's internal temperature reaches 145°F (63ºC). This same technique can be done over an open flame or in a cast-iron skillet with some butter.

5.   Remove the Tri-Tip roast from the grill and let it rest 10 to 15 minutes, before slicing and serving.

Smoked Tri-Tip Roast

Prep time: 25 minutes | Cook time: 5 hours | Serves 4

1½ pounds (680 g) Tri-Tip roast

Salt, to taste

Freshly ground black pepper, to taste

2 teaspoons garlic powder

2 teaspoons lemon pepper

½ cup apple juice

1.   Supply your Traeger with wood pellets and follow the start-up procedure. Preheat the grill, with the lid closed, to 180ºF (82ºC).

2.   Season the Tri-Tip roast with salt, pepper, garlic powder, and lemon pepper. Using your hands, work the seasoning into the meat.

3.   Place the roast directly on the grill grate and smoke for 4 hours.

4.   Pull the Tri-Tip from the grill and place it on enough aluminum foil to wrap it completely.

5.   Increase the grill's temperature to 375°F (191ºC).

6.   Fold in three sides of the foil around the roast and add the apple juice. Fold in the last side, completely enclosing the Tri-Tip and liquid. Return the wrapped Tri-Tip to the grill and cook for 45 minutes more.

7.   Remove the Tri-Tip roast from the grill and let it rest for 10 to 15 minutes, before unwrapping, slicing, and serving.

Santa Maria Tri-Tip Bottom Sirloin

Prep time: 15 minutes | Cook time: 45 minutes to 1 hour | Serves 4

2 teaspoons sea salt

2 teaspoons freshly ground black pepper

2 teaspoons onion powder

2 teaspoons garlic powder

2 teaspoons dried oregano

1 teaspoon cayenne pepper

1 teaspoon ground sage

1 teaspoon finely chopped fresh rosemary

1 (1½- to 2-pound / 680- to 907-g) tri-tip bottom sirloin

1.   Supply your Traeger with wood pellets and follow the start-up procedure. Preheat the grill, with the lid closed, to 425ºF (218ºC).

2.   In a small bowl, combine the salt, pepper, onion powder, garlic powder, oregano, cayenne pepper, sage, and rosemary to create a rub.

3.   Season the meat all over with the rub and lay it directly on the grill.

4.   Close the lid and smoke for 45 minutes to 1 hour, or until a meat thermometer inserted in the thickest part of the meat reads 120ºF (49ºC) for rare, 130ºF (54ºC) for medium-rare, or 140ºF (60ºC) for medium, keeping in mind that the meat will come up in temperature by about another 5ºF (-15ºC) during the rest period.

5.   Remove the tri-tip from the heat, tent with aluminum foil, and let rest for 15 minutes before slicing against the grain.

Mustard Pulled Beef

Prep time: 25 minutes | Cook time: 12 to 14 hours | Serves 5 to 8

1 (4-pound / 1.8-kg) top round roast

2 tablespoons yellow mustard

1 batch Espresso Brisket Rub

½ cup beef broth

1.   Supply your Traeger with wood pellets and follow the start-up procedure. Preheat the grill, with the lid closed, to 225ºF (107ºC).

2.   Coat the top round roast all over with mustard and season it with the rub. Using your hands, work the rub into the meat.

3.   Place the roast directly on the grill grate and smoke until its internal temperature reaches 160ºF (71ºC) and a dark bark has formed.

4.   Pull the roast from the grill and place it on enough aluminum foil to wrap it completely.

5.   Increase the grill's temperature to 350ºF (177ºC).

6.   Fold in three sides of the foil around the roast and add the beef broth. Fold in the last side, completely enclosing the roast and liquid. Return the wrapped roast to the grill and cook until its internal temperature reaches 195ºF (91ºC).

7.   Pull the roast from the grill and place it in a cooler. Cover the cooler and let the roast rest for 1 or 2 hours.

8.   Remove the roast from the cooler and unwrap it. Pull apart the beef using just your fingers. Serve immediately.

Smoked Top Round Roast Beef

Prep time: 10 minute | Cook time: 12 to 14 hours | Serves 5 to 8

1 (4-pound / 1.8-kg) top round roast

1 batch Espresso Brisket Rub

1 tablespoon butter

1.   Supply your Traeger with wood pellets and follow the start-up procedure. Preheat the grill, with the lid closed, to 180°F (82°C).

2.   Season the top round roast with the rub. Using your hands, work the rub into the meat.

3.   Place the roast directly on the grill grate and smoke until its internal temperature reaches 140°F (60°C). Remove the roast from the grill.

4.   Place a cast-iron skillet on the grill grate and increase the grill's temperature to 450°F (232°C). Place the roast in the skillet, add the butter, and cook until its internal temperature reaches 145°F (63°C), flipping once after about 3 minutes.

5.   Remove the roast from the grill and let it rest for 10 to 15 minutes, before slicing and serving.

Smoked Mustard Beef Ribs

Prep time: 25 minutes | Cook time: 4 to 6 hours | Serves 4 to 8

2 (2- or 3-pound / 907- or 1360-g) racks beef ribs

2 tablespoons yellow mustard

1 batch sweet and spicy cinnamon rub

1.   Supply your Traeger with wood pellets and follow the start-up procedure. Preheat the grill, with the lid closed, to 225°F (107°C).

2.   Remove the membrane from the backside of the ribs. This can be done by cutting just through the membrane in an X pattern and working a paper towel between the membrane and the ribs to pull it off.

3.   Coat the ribs all over with mustard and season them with the rub. Using your hands, work the rub into the meat.

4.   Place the ribs directly on the grill grate and smoke until their internal temperature reaches between 190°F (88°C) and 200°F (93°C).

5.   Remove the racks from the grill and cut them into individual ribs. Serve immediately.

Braised Beef Short Ribs

Prep time: 25 minutes | Cook time: 4 hours | Serves 2 to 4

4 beef short ribs

Salt, to taste

Freshly ground black pepper, to taste

½ cup beef broth

1.   Supply your Traeger with wood pellets and follow the start-up procedure. Preheat the grill, with the lid closed, to 180°F (82°C).

2.   Season the ribs on both sides with salt and pepper.

3.   Place the ribs directly on the grill grate and smoke for 3 hours.

4.   Pull the ribs from the grill and place them on enough aluminum foil to wrap them completely.

5.   Increase the grill's temperature to 375°F (191°C).

6.   Fold in three sides of the foil around the ribs and add the beef broth. Fold in the last side, completely enclosing the ribs and liquid. Return the wrapped ribs to the grill and cook for 45 minutes more. Remove the short ribs from the grill, unwrap them, and serve immediately.

Roasted Prime Rib

Prep time: 15 minutes | Cook time: 4 or 5 hours | Serves 8 to 12

1 (3-bone) rib roast

Salt, to taste

Freshly ground black pepper, to taste

1 garlic clove, minced

1.   Supply your Traeger with wood pellets and follow the start-up procedure. Preheat the grill, with the lid closed, to 360°F (182°C).

2.   Season the roast all over with salt and pepper and, using your hands, rub it all over with the minced garlic.

3.   Place the roast directly on the grill grate and smoke for 4 or 5 hours, until its internal temperature reaches 145°F (63°C) for medium-rare.

4.   Remove the roast from the grill and let it rest for 15 minutes, before slicing and serving.

Smoked Pastrami

Prep time: 15 minutes | Cook time: 12 to 16 hours | Serves 6 to 8

1 (8-pound / 3.6-kg) corned beef brisket

2 tablespoons yellow mustard

1 batch Espresso Brisket Rub

Worcestershire Mop and Spritz, for spritzing

1. Supply your Traeger with wood pellets and follow the start-up procedure. Preheat the grill, with the lid closed, to 225ºF (107ºC).

2. Coat the brisket all over with mustard and season it with the rub. Using your hands, work the rub into the meat. Pour the mop into a spray bottle.

3. Place the brisket directly on the grill grate and smoke until its internal temperature reaches 195°F (91ºC), spritzing it every hour with the mop.

4. Pull the corned beef brisket from the grill and wrap it completely in aluminum foil or butcher paper. Place the wrapped brisket in a cooler, cover the cooler, and let it rest for 1 or 2 hours.

5. Remove the corned beef from the cooler and unwrap it. Slice the corned beef and serve.

New York Steaks

Prep time: 15 minutes | Cook time: 1 to 2 hours | Serves 4

4 (1-inch-thick) New York steaks

2 tablespoons olive oil

Salt, to taste

Freshly ground black pepper, to taste

1. Supply your Traeger with wood pellets and follow the start-up procedure. Preheat the grill, with the lid closed, to 180ºF (82ºC).

2. Rub the steaks all over with olive oil and season both sides with salt and pepper.

3. Place the steaks directly on the grill grate and smoke for 1 hour.

4. Increase the grill's temperature to 375°F (191ºC) and continue to cook until the steaks' internal temperature reaches 145°F (63ºC) for medium-rare.

5. Remove the steaks and let them rest 5 minutes, before slicing and serving.

T-Bones Steak

Prep time: 10 minute | Cook time: 30 minute | Serves 4

4 (1½- to 2-inch-thick) T-bone steaks

2 tablespoons olive oil

1 batch Espresso Brisket Rub or Chili-Coffee Rub

1.   Supply your Traeger with wood pellets and follow the start-up procedure. Preheat the grill, with the lid closed, to 500ºF (260ºC).

2.   Coat the steaks all over with olive oil and season both sides with the rub. Using your hands, work the rub into the meat.

3.   Place the steaks directly on a grill grate and smoke until their internal temperature reaches 135ºF (57ºC) for rare, 145°F (63ºC) for medium-rare, and 155°F (68ºC) for well-done. Remove the steaks from the grill and serve hot.

Reverse-Seared Sirlion Steaks

Prep time: 15 minutes | Cook time: 1 or 2 hours | Serves 4

4 (4-ounce / 113-g) sirloin steaks

2 tablespoons olive oil

Salt, to taste

Freshly ground black pepper, to taste

4 tablespoons butter

1.   Supply your Traeger with wood pellets and follow the start-up procedure. Preheat the grill, with the lid closed, to 180ºF (82ºC).

2.   Rub the steaks all over with olive oil and season both sides with salt and pepper.

3.   Place the steaks directly on the grill grate and smoke until their internal temperature reaches 135ºF (57ºC). Remove the steaks from the grill.

4.   Place a cast-iron skillet on the grill grate and increase the grill's temperature to 450ºF (232ºC).

5.   Place the steaks in the skillet and top each with 1 tablespoon of butter. Cook the steaks until their internal temperature reaches 145°F (63ºC), flipping once after 2 or 3 minutes. (I recommend reverse-searing over an open flame rather than in the cast-iron skillet, if your grill has that option.) Remove the steaks and serve immediately.

Asian Sirloin Steak Skewers

Prep time: 10 minute | Cook time: 1⅓ hours | Serves 6

1½ pounds (680 g) top sirloin steak

6 garlic cloves, minced

1 red onion

⅓ cup sugar

¾ cup soy sauce

1 tablespoon ground ginger

¼ cup sesame oil

3 tablespoon sesame seeds

¼ cup vegetable oil

Bamboo skewers

1.   Cut sirloin steak into cubes, about 1 inch.

2.   Cut red onion into chunks similar in size to the sirloin steak cubes.

3.   In a bowl, combine and whisk soy sauce, sesame oil, vegetable oil, minced garlic, sugar, ginger, and sesame seeds.

4.   Add steak to sauce bowl and toss to coat until steak is covered in the sauce.

5.   Marinate for at least 1 hour in a refrigerator (if you are in a rush it's ok to skip this part, but you'll sacrifice a little bit of flavor).

6.   Preheat pellet grill to 350°F (177°C).

7.   Thread marinated beef and red onion pieces onto bamboo skewers.

8.   Grill the skewers, turning after about 4 minutes. Cook for 8 minutes total or until meat reaches your desired doneness.

Tomahawk Ribeye Steak

Prep time: 45 minutes | Cook time: 1 or 2 hours | Serves 4 to 6

1 (2½- to 3½-lbs / 1.1- to 1.6-kg) tomahawk ribeye steak

5 garlic cloves, minced

2 tablespoon kosher salt

1 bundle fresh thyme

2 tablespoon ground black pepper

8 ounces butter stick

1 tablespoon garlic powder

⅛ cup olive oil

1.   Mix rub ingredients (salt, black pepper, and garlic powder) in a small bowl. Use this mixture to season all sides of the ribeye steak generously. You can also substitute your favorite steak seasoning. After applying seasoning, let the steak rest at room temperature for at least 30 minute.

2.   While the steak rests, preheat your pellet grill to 450ºF (232ºC) to 500ºF (260ºC) for searing.

3.   Sear the steak for 5 minutes on each side. Halfway through each side (so after 2½ minutes), rotate the steak 90º to form grill marks on the tomahawk.

4.   After the tomahawk steak has seared for 5 minutes on each side (10 minute total), move the steak to a raised rack.

5.   Adjust your pellet grill's temperature to 250ºF (121ºC) and turn up smoke setting if applicable. Leave the lid open for a moment to help allow some heat to escape.

6.   Stick your probe meat thermometer into the very center of the cut to measure internal temperature.

7.   Place butter stick, garlic cloves, olive oil, and thyme in the aluminum pan. Then place the aluminum pan under the steak to catch drippings. After a few minutes, the steak drippings and ingredients will mix together

8.   Baste the steak with the aluminum pan mixture every 10 minute until the tomahawk steak reaches your desired doneness

9.   Once the steak reaches its desired doneness, remove from the grill and place on a cutting board or serving dish. The steak should rest for 10-15 minutes before cutting/serving.

Spicy Beef Tenderloin

Prep time: 25 minutes | Cook time: 1¼ hours | Serves 6

2½ pounds (1.1 kg) center cut beef tenderloin, trimmed and tied if uneven

2 tablespoon unsalted butter, room temperature

6 tablespoon peppercorns, mixed colors

1 tablespoon kosher salt

1 cup parsley, chopped

Horseradish sauce, on the side

4 tablespoon Dijon mustard

1.   Coarsely grind peppercorn mixture into a bowl. Add parsley, mustard, butter, and salt. Mix until thoroughly combined.

2.   Rub spiced butter mixture generously and thoroughly on all sides of the tenderloin. Coat completely and roll tenderloin in bowl if necessary to soak up as much seasoning as possible.

3.   Preheat pellet grill to 450ºF (232ºC).

4.   Place tenderloin on an elevated rack (important) and roast. Use a probe meat thermometer to measure internal temperature. Cook until the center of the tenderloin reaches a temperature of 130ºF (54ºC). This typically takes 30-45 minutes but could be more or less depending on the size of your tenderloin.

5.   Once tenderloin reaches desired doneness, remove from grill and allow to rest for at least 15 minutes.

6.   Move tenderloin to a cutting board and slice. Try to catch as many juices as possible. Garnish with additional parsley.

Korean Short Ribs

Prep time: 15 minutes | Cook time: 8 hours | Serves 5

3 lbs (1.4kg) beef short ribs

2 tablespoon sugar

¾ cup water

1 tablespoon ground black pepper

3 tablespoon white vinegar

2 tablespoon sesame oil

3 tablespoon soy sauce

6 cloves garlic, minced

⅓ cup light brown sugar

½ yellow onion, finely chopped

1. Combine soy sauce, water, and vinegar in a bowl. Mix and whisk in brown sugar, white sugar, pepper, sesame oil, garlic, and onion. Whisk until the sugars have completely dissolved.

2. Pour marinade into large bowl or baking pan with high sides. Dunk the short ribs in the marinade, coating completely. Cover marinaded short ribs with plastic wrap and refrigerate for 6 to 12 hours.

3. Preheat pellet grill to 225ºF (107ºC).

4. Remove plastic wrap from ribs and pull ribs out of marinade. Shake off any excess marinade and dispose of the contents left in the bowl.

5. Place ribs on grill and cook for about 6-8 hours, until ribs reach an internal temperature of 203ºF (95ºC). Measure using a probe meat thermometer.

6. Once ribs reach temperature, remove from grill and allow to rest for about 20 minute. Slice, serve, and enjoy!

Swiss Cheese Beef Meatloaf

Prep time: 15 minutes | Cook time: 2 hours | Serves 4

1 tablespoon canola oil

2 garlic cloves, finely chopped

1 medium onion, finely chopped

1 poblano chile, stemmed, seeded, and finely chopped

2 pounds extra-lean ground beef

2 tablespoons Montreal steak seasoning

1 tablespoon A.1. steak sauce

½ pound bacon, cooked and crumbled

2 cups shredded Swiss cheese

1 egg, beaten

2 cups breadcrumbs

½ cup Tiger Sauce

1.   On your stove top, heat the canola oil in a medium sauté pan over medium-high heat. Add the garlic, onion, and poblano, and sauté for 3 to 5 minutes, or until the onion is just barely translucent.

2.   Supply your smoker with wood pellets and follow the manufacturer's specific start-up procedure. Preheat, with the lid closed, to 225ºF (107ºC).

3.   In a large bowl, combine the sautéed vegetables, ground beef, steak seasoning, steak sauce, bacon, Swiss cheese, egg, and breadcrumbs. Mix with your hands until well incorporated, then shape into a loaf.

4.   Put the meatloaf in a cast iron skillet and place it on the grill. Close the lid and smoke for 2 hours, or until a meat thermometer inserted in the loaf reads 165ºF (74ºC).

5.   Top with the meatloaf with the Tiger Sauce, remove from the grill, and let rest for about 10 minute before serving.

Homemade London Broil

1 (1½- to 2-pound / 680- to 907-g) London broil or top round steak

¼ cup soy sauce

2 tablespoons white wine

2 tablespoons extra-virgin olive oil

¼ cup chopped scallions

2 tablespoons packed brown sugar

2 garlic cloves, minced

2 teaspoons red pepper flakes

1 teaspoon freshly ground black pepper

1.   Using a meat mallet, pound the steak lightly all over on both sides to break down its fibers and tenderize. You are not trying to pound down the thickness.

2.   In a medium bowl, make the marinade by combining the soy sauce, white wine, olive oil, scallions, brown sugar, garlic, red pepper flakes, and black pepper.

3.   Put the steak in a shallow plastic container with a lid and pour the marinade over the meat. Cover and refrigerate for at least 4 hours.

4.   Remove the steak from the marinade, shaking off any excess, and discard the marinade.

5.   Supply your smoker with wood pellets and follow the manufacturer's specific start-up procedure. Preheat, with the lid closed, to 350ºF (177ºC).

6.   Place the steak directly on the grill, close the lid, and smoke for 6 minutes. Flip, then smoke with the lid closed for 6 to 10 minute more, or until a meat thermometer inserted in the meat reads 130ºF (54ºC) for medium-rare.

7.   Let the steak rest for about 10 minute before slicing and serving. The meat's temperature will rise by about 5 degrees while it rests

Texas Beef Shoulder Clod

Prep time: 15 minutes | Cook time: 12 to 16 hours | Serves 16 to 20

½ cup sea salt

½ cup freshly ground black pepper

1 tablespoon red pepper flakes

1 tablespoon minced garlic

1 tablespoon cayenne pepper

1 tablespoon smoked paprika

1 (13- to 15-pound / 5.9- to 6.8-kg) beef shoulder clod

1.   In a small bowl, combine the salt, pepper, red pepper flakes, minced garlic, cayenne pepper, and smoked paprika to create a rub. Generously apply it to the beef shoulder.

2.   Supply your smoker with wood pellets and follow the manufacturer's specific start-up procedure. Preheat, with the lid closed, to 250ºF (121ºC).

3.   Put the meat on the grill grate, close the lid, and smoke for 12 to 16 hours, or until a meat thermometer inserted deeply into the beef reads 195°F (91ºC). You may need to cover the clod with aluminum foil toward the end of smoking to prevent overbrowning.

4.   Let the meat rest for about 15 minutes before slicing against the grain and serving.

Somked Cheeseburger Hand Pies

Prep time: 35 minutes | Cook time: 10 minute | Serves 4

½ pound lean ground beef

1 tablespoon minced onion

1 tablespoon steak seasoning

1 cup shredded Monterey Jack and Colby cheese blend

8 slices white American cheese, divided

2 (14-ounce / 397-g) refrigerated prepared pizza dough sheets, divided

2 eggs, beaten with 2 tablespoons water (egg wash), divided

24 hamburger dill pickle chips

2 tablespoons sesame seeds

6 slices tomato, for garnish

Ketchup and mustard, for serving

1.   Supply your smoker with wood pellets and follow the manufacturer's specific start-up procedure. Preheat, with the lid closed, to 325ºF (163ºC).

2.   On your stove top, in a medium sauté pan over medium-high heat, brown the ground beef for 4 to 5 minutes, or until cooked through. Add the minced onion and steak seasoning.

3.   Toss in the shredded cheese blend and 2 slices of American cheese, and stir until melted and fully incorporated.

4.   Remove the cheeseburger mixture from the heat and set aside.

5.   Make sure the dough is well chilled for easier handling. Working quickly, roll out one prepared pizza crust on parchment paper and brush with half of the egg wash.

6.   Arrange the remaining 6 slices of American cheese on the dough to outline 6 hand pies.

7.   Top each cheese slice with ¼ cup of the cheeseburger mixture, spreading slightly inside the imaginary lines of the hand pies.

8.   Place 4 pickle slices on top of the filling for each pie.

9.   Top the whole thing with the other prepared pizza crust and cut between the cheese slices to create 6 hand pies.

10. Using kitchen scissors, cut the parchment to further separate the pies, but leave them on the paper.

11. Using a fork dipped in egg wash, seal the edges of the pies on all sides. Baste the tops of the pies with the remaining egg wash and sprinkle with the sesame seeds.

12. Remove the pies from the parchment paper and gently place on the grill grate. Close the lid and smoke for 5 minutes, then carefully flip and smoke with the lid closed for 5 more minutes, or until browned.

13. Top with the sliced tomato and serve with ketchup and mustard.

Spiced Brisket

Prep time: 15 minutes | Cook time: 9 hours | Serves 8

Rub:

2 tablespoons onion powder

2 tablespoons garlic powder

2 teaspoons chile powder

2 tablespoons paprika

⅓ cup coarse ground black pepper

⅓ cup jacobsen salt or kosher salt

Brisket:

1 (12- to 14-pound / 5.4- to 6.4-kg) whole packer brisket, trimmed

1½ cup beef broth

1.   In a small bowl, thoroughly combine all the rub ingredients. Season the brisket with the rub on all sides.

2.   When ready to cook, set Traeger temperature to 225ºF (107ºC) and preheat, lid closed for 15 minutes. For optimal flavor, use Super Smoke if available.

3.   Place the brisket, fat-side down, on the grill and cook for about 5 to 6 hour, or until it reaches an internal temperature of 160ºF (71ºC).

4.   Remove the brisket from the grill and wrap in a double layer of foil, then add the beef broth to the foil packet.

5.   Return the foiled brisket to the grill and cook for about another 3 hours, or until it reaches an internal temperature of 204ºF (96ºC).

6.   Remove the brisket from grill and unwrap from foil. Allow to rest for 15 minutes. Slice the brisket against the grain and serve warm.

Dijon Corned Beef Brisket

Prep time: 15 minutes | Cook time: 5 hours | Serves 4

1 (3-pound / 1.4-kg) flat cut corned beef brisket, fat cap at least ¼ inch thick

¼ cup Dijon mustard

1 bottle Traeger Apricot BBQ Sauce

1.   Remove the brisket from its packaging and discard the spice packet, if any. Soak the brisket in water for at least 8 hours, changing the water every 2 hours.

2.   When ready to cook, set Traeger temperature to 275ºF (135ºC) and preheat, lid closed for 15 minutes.

3.   Place the brisket, fat-side up, directly on the grill and cook for 2 hours.

4.   Meanwhile, whisk the remaining ingredients together in a medium bowl. Pour half of the sauce mixture into the bottom of a disposable aluminum foil pan.

5.   Using tongs, transfer the brisket, fat-side up, to the pan. Pour the remaining sauce mixture over the top of the brisket, spreading the sauce evenly with a spatula. Cover the pan tightly with aluminum foil.

6.   Return the brisket to the grill and cook for an additional 2 to 3 hours, or until the brisket is tender and reaches an internal temperature of 203ºF (95ºC).

7.   Let the brisket cool for 15 to 20 minutes. Slice the brisket across the grain and serve warm.

Smoked Wagyu Tri-Tip

Prep time: 5 minutes | Cook time: 1 hour | Serves 4

1 Wagyu beef tri-tip, trimmed

½ cup Traeger Prime Rib Rub

1.   Generously season the tri-tip with Traeger Prime Rib Rub.

2.   When ready to cook, set temperature to 225ºF (107ºC) and preheat, lid closed for 15 minutes. For optimal flavor, use Super Smoke if available.

3.   Put the tri-tip on the grill and cook for 1 to 1½ hours, or until it reaches an internal temperature of 130ºF (54ºC).

4.   Remove the tri-tip from the grill and set aside.

5.   Increase the grill temperature to 475ºF (246ºC). After 15 minutes, return the tri-tip to the grill and cook each side for 3 minutes.

6.   Remove the tri-tip from the grill and slice to serve.

Brined Brisket

Prep time: 20 minutes | Cook time: 7 hours | Serves 4

1 cup brown sugar

½ cup kosher salt

1 (5- to 7-pound / 2.3- to 3.2-kg) flat cut brisket

¼ cup Traeger Beef Rub

1.   Dissolve the sugar and salt in 6 quarts boiling water. Add 6 cups ice then let it cool. Put the brisket into the brine and cover. Place the brine in the refrigerator overnight.

2.   Remove the brisket from the brine and pat dry with paper towels. Evenly sprinkle Traeger Beef Rub on the brisket.

3.   When ready to cook, set Traeger temperature to 250ºF (121ºC) and preheat, lid closed for 15 minutes.

4.   Put the brisket, fat-cap down, on the grill and smoke for 3 hours.

5.   Remove the brisket from the grill and wrap in a double layer of foil. Increase the grill temperature to 275ºF (135ºC) and cook for an additional 3 to 4 hours, or until the internal temperature reaches 204ºF (96ºC) on a meat thermometer.

6.   Unwrap the brisket and place it on the grill and cook for 30 minutes more.

7.   Remove the brisket from the grill and cool for 15 minutes before slicing against the grain and serving.

Garlic-Parmesan Crusted Filet Mignon

Prep time: 15 minutes | Cook time: 10 minutes | Serves 4

8 filet Mignon steaks

2 teaspoons garlic salt

2 teaspoons black pepper

2 teaspoons salt

2 cup grated Parmesan cheese

8 garlic, minced

2 tablespoons Dijon mustard

1.   Season the filets with garlic salt, pepper, and salt. Combine the cheese and minced garlic in a shallow bowl.

2.   When ready to cook, set Traeger temperature to High and preheat, lid closed for 15 minutes.

3.   Put the filets on the grill and cook each side for 4 minutes. When done, spread the Dijon mustard onto the filets, then dredge in the cheese-garlic mixture. Return the filets to the grill and cook for an additional 1 to 2 minutes, or until the cheese melts.

4.   Cool for 5 minutes before serving.

Coffee Rub Brisket

Prep time: 15 minutes | Cook time: 9 hours | Serves 8

15 pounds (6.8 kg) whole packer brisket

1½ cups water, divided

2 tablespoons Traeger Coffee Rub, divided

2 tablespoons salt, divided

1.   Trim the excess fat off the brisket, leaving a ¼-inch cap on the bottom.

2.   In a small bowl, mix together 1 cup of water, 1 tablespoon of rub, and 1 tablespoon of salt. Keep stirring until most of the salt is dissolved.

3.   Inject the brisket every square inch or so with the rub mixture. Season the exterior of the brisket with the remaining 1 tablespoon of rub and salt.

4.   When ready to cook, set the Traeger to 250°F (121°C) and preheat, lid closed for 15 minutes.

5.   Put the brisket directly on the grill and cook until it reaches an internal temperature of 160°F (71°C), about 6 hours.

6.   Wrap the brisket in two layers of foil and pour the remaining ½ cup of water into the foil packet. Secure tin foil tightly to contain the liquid. Increase the grill temperature to 275°F (135°C) and place the brisket back on the grill. Cook for another 3 hours, or until the internal temperature reaches 204°F (96°C).

7.   Remove the brisket from the grill and slice to serve.

Porterhouse Steaks with Creamed Greens

Prep time: 10 minutes | Cook time: 1 hour 20 minutes | Serves 4

2 Porterhouse steaks

Kosher salt and cracked black pepper, to taste

6 tablespoons butter, divided

1 shallot, thinly sliced

2 clove garlic, minced

1 cup heavy cream

1 pinch ground nutmeg

3 pounds (1.4 kg) mixed salad greens

1.   Generously season the steaks with salt and pepper on both sides.

2.   When ready to cook, set the Traeger to 225ºF (107ºC) and preheat, lid closed for 15 minutes.

3.   Put the seasoned steaks directly on the grill and cook until the internal temperature registers 120ºF (49ºC), for 45 minutes.

4.   Remove the steaks from the grill and increase the temperature to 450ºF (232ºC). Let the grill preheat with the lid closed for 15 minutes.

5.   Return the steaks to the hot grill and cook for an additional 5 to 6 minutes per side, or until the internal temperature reaches 130ºF (54ºC) for medium rare. Remove the steaks from the grill and set aside to cool.

6.   For the creamed greens: Heat 2 tablespoons of the butter in a saucepan over high heat until it foams. Add the shallot and garlic and cook over medium-low heat for about 5 minutes, stirring often, or until softened.

7.   Stir in the heavy cream and bring to a simmer. Cook for about 10 minutes until slightly thickened. Sprinkle with the nutmeg and season with salt to taste. Purée the ingredients with a hand blender until smooth. Set aside.

8.   Heat the remaining 4 tablespoons of butter in a large pot over high heat until it foams. Add the greens and cook for about 5 minutes, stirring constantly, or until they are tender but still bright green.

9.   Season as needed with salt and add the cream mixture. Reduce the heat, cover, and allow to simmer for 5 minutes more until cooked through.

10. To serve, slice the steaks and serve on top of the creamed greens.

Bacon-Onion Jam Strip Steaks

Prep time: 10 minutes | Cook time: 1 hour | Serves 2

2 whole New York strip steaks, room temperature

Traeger Prime Rib Rub, to taste

½ pound (227 g) bacon, cut into small pieces

1 small sweet onion

¼ cup brown sugar

¼ cup apple juice

3 tablespoons strong brewed coffee

½ tablespoon balsamic vinegar

Extra-virgin olive oil, as needed

1.	Season the steaks with Traeger Prime Rib Rub on both sides. Set aside.

2.	When ready to cook, start the Traeger to 350ºF (177ºC) and preheat, lid closed for 15 minutes.

3.	Put the bacon pieces in a cast iron pan and place on the hot grill. Cook for 10 to 15 minutes until the fat is rendered.

4.	Remove the bacon from the pan and drain out all but 1 tablespoon of the bacon grease from the pan.

5.	Add the onion to the cast iron pan and cook for about 10 minutes on the grill, or until the onion is tender. Add the brown sugar and cook for about another 15 to 20 minutes, or until the onion begins to caramelize.

6.	Stir in the apple juice, coffee, and cooked bacon and continue to cook for about 20 minutes, stirring occasionally.

7.	Pour in the balsamic vinegar and spoon into a bowl and set aside.

8.	Turn the heat on the Traeger to High and allow to preheat for 15 minutes with the lid closed.

9.	Lightly drizzle the olive oil over the steaks and place them on the grill. Cook each side for about 4 to 5 minutes, for medium-rare, or until cooked to your desired doneness.

10.	Remove the steaks from the grill and cool for about 10 minutes before slicing. Serve the steaks topped with the bacon-onion jam.

Texas Smoked Brisket

Prep time: 15 minutes | Cook time: 10 hours | Serves 8

1 (14- to 18-pound / 6.4- to 8.2-kg) whole packer brisket, trimmed

Meat Church Holy Cow BBQ Rub

Meat Church Holy Gospel BBQ Rub

1.   Season the brisket with Meat Church Holy Cow Rub on all sides. Optionally add a light layer of Meat Church Holy Gospel Rub. Allow the brisket to sit for 20 to 30 minutes.

2.   When ready to cook, set the Traeger temperature to 275ºF (135ºC) and preheat, lid closed for 15 minutes.

3.   Put the brisket, fat side up, on the grill and cook for about 5 to 6 hours, or until it reaches an internal temperature of 165ºF (74ºC).

4.   Remove the brisket from the grill and wrap tightly in Traeger Butcher Paper.

5.   Return the wrapped brisket to the grill and continue to cook for about 3 to 4 hours, or until it reaches an internal temperature of 204ºF (96ºC).

6.   Remove the brisket from the grill and rest for 30 minutes. Unwrap the brisket and slice against the grain before serving.

Bacon-Wrapped Tenderloin Roast

Prep time: 10 minutes | Cook time: 1 hour | Serves 4

4 pounds (1.8 kg) beef tenderloin

4 ounces (113 g) Traeger Beef Rub

4 ounces (113 g) Traeger Coffee Rub

8 strips bacon

1.   When ready to cook, set the Traeger to 275ºF (135ºC) and preheat, lid closed for 15 minutes.

2.   Lightly season the beef tenderloin with the beef rub and wrap with the bacon. Season again with another layer of coffee rub.

3.   Put the tenderloin directly on the grill and cook for 30 minutes, or until it reaches an internal temperature of 120ºF (49ºC). If not, continue to cook, checking every 5 minutes until cooked to the desired temperature.

4.   Remove the tenderloin from the grill and increase the temperature to 450ºF (232ºC).

5.   After 10 minutes, place the tenderloin back on the grill and sear for 5 minutes, or until it reaches a finished internal temperature of 135ºF (57ºC). If not, flip the tenderloin and cook for another 5 minutes.

6.   Remove the tenderloin from the grill and cool for 10 minutes before slicing and serving.

Buttered Smoked Porterhouse Steak

Prep time: 15 minutes | Cook time: 45 minutes | Serves 2

4 tablespoons butter, melted

2 teaspoons Dijon mustard

2 tablespoons Worcestershire sauce

40 ounces (1.1 kg) Porterhouse steaks

1 teaspoon Traeger Coffee Rub

1.   When ready to cook, set the Traeger to 180ºF (82ºC) and preheat, lid closed for 15 minutes. For optimal flavor, use Super Smoke if available.

2.   Whisk the melted butter, mustard, and Worcestershire sauce together in a small bowl until smooth. Brush the mixture on both sides of the steaks. Season both sides of the steaks with Traeger Coffee Rub.

3.   Place the steaks directly on the grill and smoke for 30 minutes. With tongs, transfer the steaks to a plate.

4.   Increase the grill temperature to High and preheat. For optimal results, set to 500ºF (260ºC) if available. Brush the steaks again with the butter mixture.

5.   Place the steaks back on the grill and continue to cook until the desired internal temperature is reached, 130ºF (54ºC) for medium rare, 135ºF (57ºC) for medium-well.

6.   Cool for 5 minutes before serving.

Marinated London Broil with Butter Cheese

Prep time: 10 minutes | Cook time: 1 hour 20 minutes | Serves 4

Marinade:

¼ cup water

¼ cup soy sauce

1 clove garlic, minced

1 small onion, coarsely chopped

2 tablespoons vegetable oil or extra-virgin olive oil

2 tablespoons red wine vinegar

1 tablespoon ketchup

1 teaspoon sugar

1 teaspoon Worcestershire sauce

1 teaspoon freshly ground black pepper

Steak:

1 (2-pound / 907-g) top round London broil steak

Traeger Beef Rub, as needed

Butter Cheese:

8 tablespoons butter, softened

¼ cup crumbled blue cheese

1 teaspoon Worcestershire sauce

1 scallion, minced

Freshly ground black pepper, to taste

1. Whisk all the marinade ingredients to combine in a small bowl.
2. Put the steak into a large resealable plastic bag and pour in the marinade. Let sit in the refrigerator for 6 hours to overnight.
3. Remove the steak from the refrigerator and rest to room temperature.
4. In a separate bowl, combine all the ingredients for the butter cheese and stir to mix well. Cover and refrigerate, if not using immediately.
5. When steak is at room temperature, discard the marinade and pat dry with paper towels, then season with Traeger Beef Rub on all sides.
6. When ready to cook, set the Traeger temperature to 180°F (82°C) and preheat, lid closed for 15 minutes.
7. Arrange the steak directly on the grill and smoke for 60 minutes. With tongs, transfer the steak to a platter.
8. Increase the temperature to 500°F (260°C) and preheat with the lid closed for 10 to 15 minutes.
9. Place the steak back on the grill and cook for about 15 to 20 minutes, or until the desired internal temperature is reached, 130°F (54°C) for medium-rare.
10. Let the steak rest for 5 minutes before thinly slicing on a diagonal. Serve the steak alongside the prepared butter cheese.

Grilled Bloody Mary Flank Steak

Prep time: 8 hours | Cook time: 15 minutes | Serves 4

1½ pounds (680 g) flank steak

Marinade:

2 cup Traeger Smoked Bloody Mary Mix

½ cup vodka

½ cup vegetable oil

3 clove garlic, minced

1 whole lemon or lime, juiced

1 tablespoon Worcestershire sauce

1 teaspoon celery salt

1 teaspoon coarse ground black pepper

Hot sauce, to taste

1. Whisk together all the ingredients except the steak in a small bowl until combined.

2. Place the steak in a resealable plastic bag and pour half the marinade over it. Allow to marinate for at least 6 hours or overnight. Refrigerate the remaining half of the marinade in an airtight container.

3. When ready to cook, set the Traeger temperature to High and preheat.

4. Pour the remaining marinade into a small saucepan and let simmer over medium heat until it has reduced by half. Keep warm and set aside.

5. Drain the steak and discard the marinade. Pat it dry with paper towels.

6. Arrange the steak directly on the grill and cook each side for 7 to 10 minutes.

7. Transfer the steak to a cutting board and cool for 3 minutes before thinly slicing on a sharp diagonal. Serve the steak with the warmed marinade on the side.

Smoked Tomahawk Steak

Prep time: 5 minutes | Cook time: 1 hour | Serves 4

1 (32-ounce / 907-g) bone-in Tomahawk rib-eye steak, 2 inch thick

Kosher salt, to taste

Meat Church Holy Cow BBQ Rub

3 tablespoons butter

1. Lightly season the steak on all sides with salt. Let sit at room temperature for 1 hour.

2. When ready to cook, set Traeger temperature to 225ºF (107ºC) and preheat, lid closed for 15 minutes. For optimal flavor, use Super Smoke if available.

3. Rinse the steak and pat it dry with paper towels. Liberally season both sides of the steak with Meat Church Holy Cow BBQ Rub.

4. Arrange the steak directly on the grill and cook for about 45 minutes, or until it reaches an internal temperature of 120ºF (49ºC). The cooking time depends on the thickness.

5. Remove the steak from the grill and rest for 10 minutes lightly tented with aluminum foil.

6. Meanwhile, put a cast iron skillet on the grill. Increase the grill temperature to 500ºF (260ºC).

7. Put the steak on the dry cast iron griddle and sear for 1 minute. Flip the steak and sear for 1 minute more. Doing this should bring your steak to an internal temperature of no more than 130ºF (54ºC).

8. Remove the steak and top with a generous amount of butter. Continue to cook for about 5 minutes, or until the internal temperature registers 130ºF (54ºC), for medium-rare.

9. Let the steak rest for 10 minutes before slicing and serving.

Cocoa-Rubbed Steak for Two

Prep time: 50 minutes | Cook time: 50 minutes | Serves 4

2 whole rib-eye roast, trimmed

1 cup Traeger Coffee Rub

¼ cup cocoa powder

1. Cut the roast into 2½-inch-thick steaks. Reserve 2 steaks and freeze the remaining steaks for later use.

2. Mix the Traeger Coffee rub and cocoa powder in a bowl. Season the steaks lightly with the rub mixture. Reserve the remaining rub mixture for later use. Allow the steaks to sit at room temperature for 45 minutes.

3. When ready to cook, set the Traeger to 225ºF (107ºC) and preheat, lid closed for 15 minutes.

4. Lay the steaks on the hot grill and cook for 40 minutes, flipping the steaks halfway through, or until the desired internal temperature is reached, between 105 to 110ºF (41 to 43ºC).

5. Remove the steaks from the grill and allow to rest on the counter.

6. Increase the temperature to High and preheat, lid closed for 15 minutes. For optimal results, set to 500ºF (260ºC) if available.

7. Return the steaks to the grill and cook for 8 minutes, flipping the steaks halfway through the cooking time, or until it reaches a finished temperature of 130ºF (54ºC), for medium rare.

8. Cool for 5 minutes before serving.

Smoked Rib-Eye Caps

Prep time: 5 minutes | Cook time: 45 minutes | Serves 4

1½ pounds (680 g) rib-eye cap, trimmed

2 tablespoons Traeger Beef Rub

2 tablespoons Traeger Coffee Rub

1. Cut the cap into 4 even portions and roll into steaks. Tie with butcher's twine to secure.

2. Mix both rubs in a small bowl, then lightly season the steaks with the rub mixture.

3. When ready to cook, set Traeger to 225ºF (107ºC) and preheat, lid closed for 15 minutes. For optimal flavor, use Super Smoke if available.

4. Lay the steaks directly on the grill and smoke for 30 to 45 minutes, or until the internal temperature reaches 120ºF (49ºC).

5. Remove the steaks from the grill and set aside to rest.

6. Increase the grill temperature to 450ºF (232ºC). Return the steaks to the grill and cook each side for 3 to 4 minutes, or until the internal temperature reaches 130ºF (54ºC).

7. Remove the steaks from the grill. Rest for 5 minutes and serve.

Spiced Tomahawk Steaks

Prep time: 5 minutes | Cook time: 1 hour | Serves 4

2 tablespoons ground black pepper

2 tablespoons kosher salt

1 tablespoon paprika

½ tablespoon brown sugar

½ tablespoon onion powder

½ tablespoon garlic powder

1 teaspoon ground mustard

¼ teaspoon cayenne pepper

2 large Tomahawk steaks

1.   Stir together all the ingredients except the steaks in a small bowl. Liberally season the steaks with the rub mixture.

2.   When ready to cook, set Traeger temperature to 225°F (107°C) and preheat, lid closed for 15 minutes. For optimal flavor, use Super Smoke if available.

3.   Arrange the steaks directly on the grill and smoke until the internal temperature reaches 120°F (49°C), 45 minutes to 1 hour.

4.   Remove the steaks from the grill and set aside to rest.

5.   Increase the grill temperature to 450°F (232°C). Return the steaks to the grill and cook each side for 7 to 10 minutes, or until the internal temperature registers 130°F (54°C).

6.   Remove the steaks from the grill cool for 5 minutes before serving.

Beef Tenderloin with Cherry Tomato Vinaigrette

Prep time: 10 minutes | Cook time: 40 minutes | Serves 6

1 whole beef tenderloin

Extra-virgin olive oil, as needed

1 bottle Traeger Prime Rib Rub

Salt and pepper, to taste

Vinaigrette:

6 whole plum tomatoes

2 tablespoons balsamic vinegar

1 teaspoon thyme, minced

1. When ready to cook, set the temperature to 450ºF (232ºC) and preheat, lid closed for 15 minutes.
2. Tuck the thin end of the tenderloin underneath the roast and secure it with butcher's string. Rub the tenderloin with olive oil and season both sides with Prime Rib Rub or salt and pepper. Put the tenderloin on a rack in a shallow roasting pan.
3. Place the pan with the tenderloin on the preheated grill and roast for 20 minutes.
4. Adjust the temperature to 350ºF (177ºC) and roast for an additional 20 minutes until cooked to the desired doneness, 130ºF (54ºC) for medium rare, 140ºF (60ºC) for medium or 150ºF (66ºC) for well done.
5. Meanwhile, make the vinaigrette by combining the tomatoes, balsamic vinegar, olive oil, and thyme in a food processor. Pulse until smoothly puréed. Season with Prime Rib Rub or salt and pepper to taste.
6. Remove the tenderloin from the grill and serve with the vinaigrette.

Grilled Beef Short Ribs

Prep time: 15 minutes | Cook time: 8 to 10 hours | Serves 8

4 (4-bone) beef short rib racks, membrane removed

½ cup Traeger Beef Rub

1 cup apple juice

1. Season the ribs with Traeger Beef Rub on both sides.
2. When ready to cook, set Traeger temperature to 225ºF (107ºC) and preheat, lid closed for 15 minutes.
3. Place the ribs, bone-side down, on the grill and cook for 8 to 10 hours, spritzing or mopping with apple juice every 60 minutes, or until the internal temperature reaches 205ºF (96ºC).
4. Remove the ribs from the grill and let rest for 5 minutes before slicing and serving.

Smoked Beef Brisket with Mop Sauce

Prep time: 15 minutes | Cook time: 12 hours | Serves 4

1 (6-pound / 2.7-kg) flat cut brisket, trimmed

Traeger Beef Rub, as needed

Traeger Texas Spicy BBQ Sauce, for serving

Mop Sauce:

2 cup beef broth

2 tablespoons Worcestershire sauce

¼ cup apple cider vinegar, apple cider or apple juice

1.   When ready to cook, set Traeger temperature to 180°F (82°C) and preheat, lid closed for 15 minutes.

2.   Season the brisket with Traeger Beef Rub on both sides. Whisk all the mop sauce ingredients together in a spray bottle.

3.   Place the brisket, fat-side down, on the grill and smoke for 3 to 4 hours, spraying the brisket with the mop sauce every hour.

4.   Remove the brisket from the grill and increase the temperature to 225°F (107°C).

5.   Place the brisket back on the grill and continue to cook for about 6 to 8 hours, spraying occasionally with the mop sauce, or until an instant-read thermometer inserted in the thickest part of the meat registers 204°F (96°C).

6.   Wrap the brisket with foil and allow to rest for 30 minutes. Slice the brisket across the grain and serve alongside the BBQ Sauce.

Steak Skewers with Cherry BBQ Sauce

Prep time: 20 minutes | Cook time: 25 minutes | Serves 4

2 tablespoons butter

1 medium onion, chopped

2 clove garlic, minced

2 cup fresh or frozen dark sweet cherries, pitted and coarsely chopped

1 cup ketchup

¼ cup cider vinegar

⅔ cup brown sugar

1 tablespoon Worcestershire sauce

½ teaspoon pepper

2 teaspoons ground mustard

1½ pounds (680 g) flank steak, cut into about 16 slices

Olive oil, as needed

Traeger Prime Rib Rub, to taste

Chopped scallions, for serving

1.   Melt the butter in a large saucepan over medium heat. Add the onion and sauté for 2 minutes until softened. Add the garlic and cook for 1 minute more.

2.   Add the cherries, ketchup, vinegar, brown sugar, Worcestershire sauce, pepper, and mustard and stir well. Cook, uncovered, over medium-low heat for 20 minutes, stirring occasionally, or until the cherries are softened and the sauce has thickened.

3.   Carefully stab each slice of steak through the center, lengthwise, with a Traeger skewer. Using a meat pounder, smash each steak skewer until about ½ inch thick.

4.   Drizzle the beef skewers with olive oil and season with Prime Rib Rub on both sides.

5.   When ready to cook, set the temperature to High and preheat, lid closed for 10 to 15 minutes.

6.   Arrange the steak skewers on the grill and cook each side for about 1 to 2 minutes.

7.   Remove the steak skewers from the grill and let rest for 5 to 10 minutes. Use a spoon to mash the cherries in the sauce. Brush the steak with the cherry barbecue sauce and serve sprinkled with the chopped scallions.

Seared Strip Steak with Butter

Prep time: 15 minutes | Cook time: 1 hour 10 minutes | Serves 4

4 (1½ inch thick) New York strip steaks

Traeger Beef Rub, as needed

4 tablespoons butter, melted

1.   When ready to cook, set Traeger temperature to 225ºF (107ºC) and preheat, lid closed for 15 minutes. For optimal flavor, use Super Smoke if available.

2.   Season the steaks with Traeger Beef Rub.

3.   Arrange the steaks directly on the grill and smoke for 60 minutes, or until they reach an internal temperature of 105 to 110ºF (41 to 43ºC).

4.   Remove the steaks from the grill and set aside to rest.

5.   Increase the grill temperature to 500ºF (260ºC) and preheat, lid closed for 15 minutes.

6.   Place the steaks back on the grill and sear for 4 minutes. Flip the steaks and spread 1 tablespoon of melted butter onto each steak. Continue to sear for 4 minutes more, or until cooked to the desired temperature, 130ºF (54ºC) to 135ºF (57ºC) for medium-rare.

7.   Remove the steaks from the grill and cool for 5 minutes before serving.

Seared Rib-Eye Steaks

Prep time: 5 minutes | Cook time: 50 minutes | Serves 2

2 (1½ inch thick) rib-eye steaks

Meat Church Gourmet Garlic and Herb Seasoning

Meat Church Holy Cow BBQ Rub

2 tablespoons butter

1.   When ready to cook, set Traeger temperature to 225ºF (107ºC) and preheat, lid closed for 15 minutes. For optimal flavor, use Super Smoke if available.

2.   Season the steaks on both sides with the seasoning and rub.

3.   Arrange the steaks on the grill and cook for 30 to 45 minutes, or until an instant-read thermometer inserted in the thickest part of the meat registers 120ºF (49ºC).

4.   Remove the steaks from the grill and set aside to cool.

5.   Increase the grill temperature to 500ºF (260ºC) and return the steaks to the grill and sear for 3 minutes.

6.   Remove the steaks from the grill and top with the butter. Lightly tent the steaks with foil to melt the butter. Cool for 5 minutes before slicing and slicing.

Garlic-Mustard Roasted Prime Rib

Prep time: 15 minutes | Cook time: 4 hours | Serves 6

1 (8- to 10-pounds / 3.6- to 4.5-kg) 4-bone prime rib roast, trimmed

4 clove garlic, mashed to a paste

3 tablespoons Dijon mustard

2 tablespoons Worcestershire sauce

2 teaspoons dried rosemary

2 teaspoons dried thyme

Coarse salt and freshly ground black pepper, to taste

Prepared horseradish, for serving (optional)

1.   Tie the prime rib roast between the bones with butcher's twine.

2.   Stir together the garlic, mustard, Worcestershire sauce, rosemary, and thyme in a small bowl until well incorporated.

3.   Slather the outside of the prime rib roast with the garlic mixture and generously season both sides with salt and black pepper. Place the prime rib roast in the refrigerator, uncovered, for up to 8 hours.

4.   When ready to cook, set Traeger temperature to 250ºF (121ºC) and preheat, lid closed for 15 minutes.

5.   Arrange the prime rib, fat-side up, on the grill and roast for 3½ to 4 hours, or until the internal temperature of the meat (the tip of the temperature probe should be in the center of the meat) registers 120ºF (49ºC) for rare, 130ºF (54ºC) for medium rare.

6.   Transfer the prime rib to a cutting board and loosely tent with foil. Let rest for 30 minutes.

7.   When ready, remove the twine. Using a sharp knife, remove the rack of bone following the curvature of the meat. Carve the meat across the grain into ½-inch-thick slices. Serve the meat alongside the horseradish, if desired.

Barbecue Baby Back Ribs

Prep time: 15 minutes | Cook time: 5 to 6 hours | Serves 12 to 15

2 full slabs baby back ribs, back membranes removed

1 cup prepared table mustard

1 cup Pork Rub

1 cup apple juice, divided

1 cup packed light brown sugar, divided

1 cup of The Ultimate BBQ Sauce, divided

1. Supply your Traeger with wood pellets and follow the manufacturer's specific start-up procedure. Preheat, with the lid closed, to 150°F (66ºC) to 180ºF (82ºC), or to the "Smoke" setting.

2. Coat the ribs with the mustard to help the rub stick and lock in moisture.

3. Generously apply the rub.

4. Place the ribs directly on the grill, close the lid, and smoke for 3 hours5. Increase the temperature to 225ºF (107ºC).

5. Remove the ribs from the grill and wrap each rack individually with aluminum foil, but before sealing tightly, add ½ cup apple juice and ½ cup brown sugar to each package.

6. Return the foil-wrapped ribs to the grill, close the lid, and smoke for 2 more hours.

7. Carefully unwrap the ribs and remove the foil completely. Coat each slab with ½ cup of barbecue sauce and continue smoking with the lid closed for 30 minute to 1 hour, or until the meat tightens and has a reddish bark. For the perfect rack, the internal temperature should be 190°F (88ºC).

Maple Baby Back Ribs

Prep time: 25 minutes | Cook time: 4 hours | Serves 4 to 6

2 (2- or 3-pound / 907- or 1360-g) racks baby back ribs

2 tablespoons yellow mustard

1 batch Sweet Brown Sugar Rub

½ cup plus 2 tablespoons maple syrup, divided

2 tablespoons light brown sugar

1 cup Pepsi or other non-diet cola

¼ cup The Ultimate BBQ Sauce

1.   Supply your smoker with wood pellets and follow the manufacturer's specific start-up procedure. Preheat the grill, with the lid closed, to 180ºF (82ºC).

2.   Remove the membrane from the backside of the ribs. This can be done by cutting just through the membrane in an X pattern and working a paper towel between the membrane and the ribs to pull it off.

3.   Coat the ribs on both sides with mustard and season them with the rub. Using your hands, work the rub into the meat.

4.   Place the ribs directly on the grill grate and smoke for 3 hours.

5.   Remove the ribs from the grill and place them, bone-side up, on enough aluminum foil to wrap the ribs completely. Drizzle 2 tablespoons of maple syrup over the ribs and sprinkle them with 1 tablespoon of brown sugar. Flip the ribs and repeat the maple syrup and brown sugar application on the meat side.

6.   Increase the grill's temperature to 300ºF (149ºC).

7.   Fold in three sides of the foil around the ribs and add the cola. Fold in the last side, completely enclosing the ribs and liquid. Return the ribs to the grill and cook for 30 to 45 minutes.

8.   Remove the ribs from the grill and unwrap them from the foil.

9.   In a small bowl, stir together the barbecue sauce and remaining 6 tablespoons of maple syrup. Use this to baste the ribs. Return the ribs to the grill, without the foil, and cook for 15 minutes to caramelize the sauce.

10. Cut into individual ribs and serve immediately.

CHAPTER 6 POULTRY

Beer Can Chicken

Prep time: 30 minute | Cook time: 3 to 4 hours | Serves 3 to 4

8 tablespoons (1 stick) unsalted butter, melted

½ cup apple cider vinegar

½ cup Cajun seasoning, divided

1 teaspoon garlic powder

1 teaspoon onion powder

1 (4-pound / 1.8-kg) whole chicken, giblets removed

Extra-virgin olive oil, for rubbing

1 (12-ounce / 340-g) can beer

1 cup apple juice

½ cup extra-virgin olive oil

1. In a small bowl, whisk together the butter, vinegar, ¼ cup of Cajun seasoning, garlic powder, and onion powder.

2. Use a meat-injecting syringe to inject the liquid into various spots in the chicken. Inject about half of the mixture into the breasts and the other half throughout the rest of the chicken.

3. Rub the chicken all over with olive oil and apply the remaining ¼ cup of Cajun seasoning, being sure to rub under the skin as well.

4. Drink or discard half the beer and place the opened beer can on a stable surface.

5. Place the bird's cavity on top of the can and position the chicken so it will sit up by itself. Prop the legs forward to make the bird more stable, or buy an inexpensive, specially made stand to hold the beer can and chicken in place.

6. Supply your smoker with wood pellets and follow the manufacturer's specific start-up procedure. Preheat, with the lid closed, to 250ºF (121ºC).

7. In a clean 12-ounce spray bottle, combine the apple juice and olive oil. Cover and shake the mop sauce well before each use.

8. Carefully put the chicken on the grill. Close the lid and smoke the chicken for 3 to 4 hours, spraying with the mop sauce every hour, until golden brown and a meat thermometer inserted in the thickest part of the thigh reads 165ºF (74ºC). Keep a piece of aluminum foil handy to loosely cover the chicken if the skin begins to brown too quickly.

9. Let the meat rest for 5 minutes before carving.

Buffalo Chicken Tortilla

Prep time: 30 minute | Cook time: 20 minute | Serves 4

2 teaspoons poultry seasoning

1 teaspoon freshly ground black pepper

1 teaspoon garlic powder

1 to 1½ pounds chicken tenders

4 tablespoons (½ stick) unsalted butter, melted

½ cup hot sauce (such as Frank's RedHot)

4 (10-inch) flour tortillas

1 cup shredded lettuce

½ cup diced tomato

½ cup diced celery

½ cup diced red onion

½ cup shredded Cheddar cheese

¼ cup blue cheese crumbles

¼ cup prepared ranch dressing

2 tablespoons sliced pickled jalapeño peppers (optional)

1.   Supply your smoker with wood pellets and follow the manufacturer's specific start-up procedure. Preheat, with the lid closed, to 350ºF (177ºC).

2.   In a small bowl, stir together the poultry seasoning, pepper, and garlic powder to create an all-purpose rub, and season the chicken tenders with it.

3.   Arrange the tenders directly on the grill, close the lid, and smoke for 20 minute, or until a meat thermometer inserted in the thickest part of the meat reads 170ºF (77ºC).

4.   In another bowl, stir together the melted butter and hot sauce and coat the smoked chicken with it.

5.   To serve, heat the tortillas on the grill for less than a minute on each side and place on a plate.

6.   Top each tortilla with some of the lettuce, tomato, celery, red onion, Cheddar cheese, blue cheese crumbles, ranch dressing, and jalapeños (if using).

7.   Divide the chicken among the tortillas, close up securely, and serve.

Smoked Whole Chicken

Prep time: 15 minutes | Cook time: 1 to 2 hours | Serves 6 to 8

1 whole chicken

2 tablespoons olive oil

1 batch chicken rub

1. Supply your smoker with wood pellets and follow the manufacturer's specific start-up procedure. Preheat the grill, with the lid closed, to 375°F (191°C).

2. Coat the chicken all over with olive oil and season it with the rub. Using your hands, work the rub into the meat.

3. Place the chicken directly on the grill grate and smoke until its internal temperature reaches 170°F (77°C).

4. Remove the chicken from the grill and let it rest for 10 minute, before carving and serving.

Tea Injectable Chicken

Prep time: 25 minutes | Cook time: 4 hours | Serves 6 to 8

1 whole chicken

2 cups tea injectable (using not-just-for-pork rub)

2 tablespoons olive oil

1 batch chicken rub

2 tablespoons butter, melted

1. Supply your smoker with wood pellets and follow the manufacturer's specific start-up procedure. Preheat the grill, with the lid closed, to 180°F (82°C).

2. Inject the chicken throughout with the tea injectable.

3. Coat the chicken all over with olive oil and season it with the rub. Using your hands, work the rub into the meat.

4. Place the chicken directly on the grill grate and smoke for 3 hours.

5. Baste the chicken with the butter and increase the grill's temperature to 375°F (191°C). Continue to cook the chicken until its internal temperature reaches 170°F (77°C).

6. Remove the chicken from the grill and let it rest for 10 minute, before carving and serving.

Smoked Skinless Chicken Breast

Prep time: 15 minutes | Cook time: 1½ hours | Serves 4 to 6

2½ pounds (1.1 kg) boneless, skinless chicken breasts

Salt, to taste

Freshly ground black pepper, to taste

1. Supply your smoker with wood pellets and follow the manufacturer's specific start-up procedure. Preheat the grill, with the lid closed, to 180ºF (82ºC).

2. Season the chicken breasts all over with salt and pepper.

3. Place the breasts directly on the grill grate and smoke for 1 hour.

4. Increase the grill's temperature to 325ºF (163ºC) and continue to cook until the chicken's internal temperature reaches 170ºF (77ºC). Remove the breasts from the grill and serve immediately.

Smoked Chicken Breast

Prep time: 10 minute | Cook time: 45 minutes | Serves 2 to 4

2 (1-pound / 454-g) bone-in, skin-on chicken breasts

1 batch Chicken Rub

1. Supply your smoker with wood pellets and follow the manufacturer's specific start-up procedure. Preheat the grill, with the lid closed, to 350ºF (177ºC).

2. Season the chicken breasts all over with the rub. Using your hands, work the rub into the meat.

3. Place the breasts directly on the grill grate and smoke until their internal temperature reaches 170ºF (77ºC). Remove the breasts from the grill and serve immediately.

Chicken Breast Tenders

Prep time: 15 minutes | Cook time: 1⅓ hours | Serves 2 to 4

1 pound (454 g) boneless, skinless chicken breast tenders

1 batch Chicken Rub

1. Supply your smoker with wood pellets and follow the manufacturer's specific start-up procedure. Preheat the grill, with the lid closed, to 180ºF (82ºC).

2. Season the chicken tenders with the rub. Using your hands, work the rub into the meat.

3. Place the tenders directly on the grill grate and smoke for 1 hour.

4. Increase the grill's temperature to 300ºF (149ºC) and continue to cook until the tenders' internal temperature reaches 170ºF (77ºC). Remove the tenders from the grill and serve immediately.

Buffalo Chicken Wings

Prep time: 15 minutes | Cook time: 35 minutes | Serves 2 to 3

1 pound (454 g) chicken wings

1 batch Chicken Rub

1 cup Frank's Red-Hot Sauce, Buffalo wing sauce, or similar

1.   Supply your smoker with wood pellets and follow the manufacturer's specific start-up procedure. Preheat the grill, with the lid closed, to 300°F (149°C).

2.   Season the chicken wings with the rub. Using your hands, work the rub into the meat.

3.   Place the wings directly on the grill grate and smoke until their internal temperature reaches 160°F (71°C).

4.   Baste the wings with the sauce and continue to smoke until the wings' internal temperature reaches 170°F (77°C).

Cinnamon Rub Chicken Wings

Prep time: 20 minute | Cook time: 1½ hours | Serves 2 to 4

1 pound (454 g) chicken wings

1 batch sweet and spicy cinnamon rub

1 cup barbecue sauce

1.   Supply your smoker with wood pellets and follow the manufacturer's specific start-up procedure. Preheat the grill, with the lid closed, to 325°F (163°C).

2.   Season the chicken wings with the rub. Using your hands, work the rub into the meat.

3.   Place the wings directly on the grill grate and cook until they reach an internal temperature of 165°F (74°C).

4.   Transfer the wings into an aluminum pan. Add the barbecue sauce and stir to coat the wings.

5.   Reduce the grill's temperature to 250°F (121°C) and put the pan on the grill. Smoke the wings for 1 hour more, uncovered. Remove the wings from the grill and serve immediately.

Smoked Chicken Drumsticks

Prep time: minutes | Cook time: | Serves

1 pound (454 g) chicken drumsticks

2 tablespoons olive oil

1 batch sweet and spicy cinnamon rub

1.   Supply your smoker with wood pellets and follow the manufacturer's specific start-up procedure. Preheat the grill, with the lid closed, to 350°F (177°C).

2.   Coat the drumsticks all over with olive oil and season with the rub. Using your hands, work the rub into the meat.

3.   Place the drumsticks directly on the grill grate and smoke until their internal temperature reaches 170°F (77°C). Remove the drumsticks from the grill and serve immediately.

Smoked Chicken Quarters

Prep time: 15 minutes | Cook time: 2 hours | Serves 2 to 4

4 chicken quarters

2 tablespoons olive oil

1 batch Chicken Rub

2 tablespoons butter

1.   Supply your smoker with wood pellets and follow the manufacturer's specific start-up procedure. Preheat the grill, with the lid closed, to 180°F (82°C).

2.   Coat the chicken quarters all over with olive oil and season them with the rub. Using your hands, work the rub into the meat.

3.   Place the quarters directly on the grill grate and smoke for 1½ hours.

4.   Baste the quarters with the butter and increase the grill's temperature to 375°F (191°C). Continue to cook until the chicken's internal temperature reaches 170°F (77°C).

5.   Remove the quarters from the grill and let them rest for 10 minute before serving.

Mandarin Glazed Whole Duck

Prep time: 20 minute | Cook time: 4 hours | Serves 4

1 quart buttermilk

1 (5-pound / 2.3-kg) whole duck

¾ cup soy sauce

½ cup hoisin sauce

½ cup rice wine vinegar

2 tablespoons sesame oil

1 tablespoon freshly ground black pepper

1 tablespoon minced garlic

Mandarin Glaze, for drizzling

1.   With a very sharp knife, remove as much fat from the duck as you can. Refrigerate or freeze the fat for later use.

2.   Pour the buttermilk into a large container with a lid and submerge the whole duck in it. Cover and let brine in the refrigerator for 4 to 6 hours.

3.   Supply your smoker with wood pellets and follow the manufacturer's specific start-up procedure. Preheat, with the lid closed, to 250ºF (121ºC).

4.   Remove the duck from the buttermilk brine, then rinse it and pat dry with paper towels.

5.   In a bowl, combine the soy sauce, hoisin sauce, vinegar, sesame oil, pepper, and garlic to form a paste. Reserve ¼ cup for basting.

6.   Poke holes in the skin of the duck and rub the remaining paste all over and inside the cavity.

7.   Place the duck on the grill breast-side down, close the lid, and smoke for about 4 hours, basting every hour with the reserved paste, until a meat thermometer inserted in the thickest part of the meat reads 165ºF (74ºC) Use aluminum foil to tent the duck in the last 30 minute or so if it starts to brown too quickly.

8.   To finish, drizzle with glaze.

Roast Whole Chicken

Prep time: 10 minute | Cook time: 1 to 2 hours | Serves 4

1 (4-pound / 1.8-kg) whole chicken, giblets removed

Extra-virgin olive oil, for rubbing

3 tablespoons Greek seasoning

Juice of 1 lemon

Butcher's string

1.   Supply your smoker with wood pellets and follow the manufacturer's specific start-up procedure. Preheat, with the lid closed, to 450ºF (232ºC).

2.   Rub the bird generously all over with oil, including inside the cavity.

3.   Sprinkle the Greek seasoning all over and under the skin of the bird, and squeeze the lemon juice over the breast.

4.   Tuck the chicken wings behind the back and tie the legs together with butcher's string or cooking twine.

5.   Put the chicken directly on the grill, breast-side up, close the lid, and roast for 1 hour to 1 hour 30 minute, or until a meat thermometer inserted in the thigh reads 165ºF (74ºC).

6.   Let the meat rest for 10 minute before carving.

Cheesy Chicken Enchiladas

Prep time: 15 minutes | Cook time: 45 minutes | Serves 6

6 cups diced cooked chicken

3 cups grated Monterey Jack cheese, divided

1 cup sour cream

1 (4-ounce / 113-g) can chopped green chiles

2 (10-ounce / 283-g) cans red or green enchilada sauce, divided

12 (8-inch) flour tortillas

½ cup chopped scallions

¼ cup chopped fresh cilantro

1. Supply your smoker with wood pellets and follow the manufacturer's specific start-up procedure. Preheat, with the lid closed, to 350°F (177°C).

2. In a large bowl, combine the cooked chicken, 2 cups of cheese, the sour cream, and green chiles to make the filling.

3. Pour one can of enchilada sauce in the bottom of a 9-by-13-inch baking dish or aluminum pan.

4. Spoon ⅓ cup of the filling on each tortilla and roll up securely.

5. Transfer the tortillas seam-side down to the baking dish, then pour the remaining can of enchilada sauce over them, coating all exposed surfaces of the tortillas.

6. Sprinkle the remaining 1 cup of cheese over the enchiladas and cover tightly with aluminum foil.

7. Bake on the grill, with the lid closed, for 30 minute, then remove the foil.

8. Continue baking with the lid closed for 15 minutes, or until bubbly.

9. Garnish the enchiladas with the chopped scallions and cilantro and serve immediately.

Cajun Turducken Roulade

Prep time: 20 minute | Cook time: 2 hours | Serves 6

1 (16-ounce / 454-g) boneless turkey breast

1 (8-to 10-ounce / 227-to 283-g) boneless duck breast

1 (8-ounce / 227-g) boneless, skinless chicken breast

Salt, to taste

Freshly ground black pepper, to taste

2 cups Italian dressing

2 tablespoons Cajun seasoning

1 cup prepared seasoned stuffing mix

8 slices bacon

Butcher's string

1. Butterfly the turkey, duck, and chicken breasts, cover with plastic wrap and, using a mallet, flatten each ½ inch thick.

2. Season all the meat on both sides with a little salt and pepper.

3. In a medium bowl, combine the Italian dressing and Cajun seasoning. Spread one-fourth of the mixture on top of the flattened turkey breast.

4. Place the duck breast on top of the turkey, spread it with one-fourth of the dressing mixture, and top with the stuffing mix.

5. Place the chicken breast on top of the duck and spread with one-fourth of the dressing mixture.

6. Supply your smoker with wood pellets and follow the manufacturer's specific start-up procedure. Preheat, with the lid closed, to 275ºF (135ºC).

7. Tightly roll up the stack, tie with butcher's string, and slather the whole thing with the remaining dressing mixture.

8. Wrap the bacon slices around the turducken and secure with toothpicks, or try making a bacon weave (see the technique for this in the Jalapeño-Bacon Pork Tenderloin recipe).

9. Place the turducken roulade in a roasting pan. Transfer to the grill, close the lid, and roast for 2 hours, or until a meat thermometer inserted in the turducken reads 165ºF (74ºC). Tent with aluminum foil in the last 30 minute, if necessary, to keep from overbrowning.

10. Let the turducken rest for 15 to 20 minute before carving. Serve warm.

Roasted Chicken Thighs

Prep time: 5 minutes | Cook time: 1 to 2 hours | Serves 12 to 15

3 pounds (1.4kg) chicken thighs

2 teaspoons salt

2 teaspoons freshly ground black pepper

2 teaspoons garlic powder

2 teaspoons onion powder

2 cups prepared Italian dressing

1.   Place the chicken thighs in a shallow dish and sprinkle with the salt, pepper, garlic powder, and onion powder, being sure to get under the skin.

2.   Cover with the Italian dressing, coating all sides, and refrigerate for 1 hour.

3.   Supply your smoker with wood pellets and follow the manufacturer's specific start-up procedure. Preheat, with the lid closed, to 250ºF (121ºC).

4.   Remove the chicken thighs from the marinade and place directly on the grill, skin-side down. Discard the marinade.

5.   Close the lid and roast the chicken for 1 hour 30 minute to 2 hours, or until a meat thermometer inserted in the thickest part of the thighs reads 165ºF (74ºC). Do not turn the thighs during the smoking process.

Mandarin Glazed Smoked Turkey Legs

Prep time: 15 minutes | Cook time: 4 to 5 hours | Serves 4

1 gallon hot water

1 cup curing salt (such as Morton Tender Quick)

¼ cup packed light brown sugar

1 teaspoon freshly ground black pepper

1 teaspoon ground cloves

1 bay leaf

2 teaspoons liquid smoke

4 turkey legs

Mandarin Glaze, for serving

1. In a large container with a lid, stir together the water, curing salt, brown sugar, pepper, cloves, bay leaf, and liquid smoke until the salt and sugar are dissolved; let come to room temperature.

2. Submerge the turkey legs in the seasoned brine, cover, and refrigerate overnight.

3. When ready to smoke, remove the turkey legs from the brine and rinse them; discard the brine.

4. Supply your smoker with wood pellets and follow the manufacturer's specific start-up procedure. Preheat, with the lid closed, to 225ºF (107ºC).

5. Arrange the turkey legs on the grill, close the lid, and smoke for 4 to 5 hours, or until dark brown and a meat thermometer inserted in the thickest part of the meat reads 165ºF (74ºC).

6. Serve with Mandarin Glaze on the side or drizzled over the turkey legs.

Jamaican Jerk Chicken Leg Quarters

Prep time: 15 minutes | Cook time: 1 to 2 hours | Serves 4

4 chicken leg quarters, scored

¼ cup canola oil

½ cup Jamaican Jerk Paste

1 tablespoon whole allspice (pimento) berries

1. Supply your smoker with wood pellets and follow the manufacturer's specific start-up procedure. Preheat, with the lid closed, to 275ºF (135ºC).

2. Brush the chicken with canola oil, then brush 6 tablespoons of the Jerk paste on and under the skin. Reserve the remaining 2 tablespoons of paste for basting.

3. Throw the whole allspice berries in with the wood pellets for added smoke flavor.

4. Arrange the chicken on the grill, close the lid, and smoke for 1 hour to 1 hour 30 minute, or until a meat thermometer inserted in the thickest part of the thigh reads 165ºF (74ºC).

5. Let the meat rest for 5 minutes and baste with the reserved jerk paste prior to serving.

Smo-Fried Spiced Chicken

Prep time: 30 minute | Cook time: 55 minutes | Serves 4 to 6

1 egg, beaten

½ cup milk

1 cup all-purpose flour

2 tablespoons salt

1 tablespoon freshly ground black pepper

2 teaspoons freshly ground white pepper

2 teaspoons cayenne pepper

2 teaspoons garlic powder

2 teaspoons onion powder

1 teaspoon smoked paprika

8 tablespoons (1 stick) unsalted butter, melted

1 whole chicken, cut up into pieces

1.   Supply your smoker with wood pellets and follow the manufacturer's specific start-up procedure. Preheat, with the lid closed, to 375°F (191ºC).

2.   In a medium bowl, combine the beaten egg with the milk and set aside.

3.   In a separate medium bowl, stir together the flour, salt, black pepper, white pepper, cayenne, garlic powder, onion powder, and smoked paprika.

4.   Line the bottom and sides of a high-sided metal baking pan with aluminum foil to ease cleanup.

5.   Pour the melted butter into the prepared pan.

6.   Dip the chicken pieces one at a time in the egg mixture, and then coat well with the seasoned flour. Transfer to the baking pan.

7.   Smoke the chicken in the pan of butter("smo-fry") on the grill, with the lid closed, for 25 minutes, then reduce the heat to 325°F and turn the chicken pieces over.

8.   Continue smoking with the lid closed for about 30 minute, or until a meat thermometer inserted in the thickest part of each chicken piece reads 165ºF (74ºC).

9.   Serve immediately.

Grilled Apple Turkey

Prep time: 10 minute | Cook time: 5 to 6 hours | Serves 6 to 8

•

1 (10- to 12-pound / 4.5- to 5.4-kg) turkey, giblets removed

Extra-virgin olive oil, for rubbing

¼ cup poultry seasoning

8 tablespoons (1 stick) unsalted butter, melted

½ cup apple juice

2 teaspoons dried sage

2 teaspoons dried thyme

1.   Supply your smoker with wood pellets and follow the manufacturer's specific start-up procedure. Preheat, with the lid closed, to 250ºF (121ºC).

2.   Rub the turkey with oil and season with the poultry seasoning inside and out, getting under the skin.

3.   In a bowl, combine the melted butter, apple juice, sage, and thyme to use for basting.

4.   Put the turkey in a roasting pan, place on the grill, close the lid, and grill for 5 to 6 hours, basting every hour, until the skin is brown and crispy, or until a meat thermometer inserted in the thickest part of the thigh reads 165ºF (74ºC).

5.   Let the bird rest for 15 to 20 minute before carving.

Teriyaki Chicken Breast

Prep time: 20 minute | Cook time: 1 to 2 hours | Serves 4

•

2 boneless chicken breasts with drumettes attached

½ cup soy sauce

½ cup teriyaki sauce

¼ cup canola oil

¼ cup white vinegar

1 tablespoon minced garlic

¼ cup chopped scallions

2 teaspoons freshly ground black pepper

1 teaspoon ground mustard

1.   Place the chicken in a baking dish.

2.   In a bowl, whisk together the soy sauce, teriyaki sauce, canola oil, vinegar, garlic, scallions, pepper and ground mustard, then pour this marinade over the chicken, coating both sides.

3.   Refrigerate the chicken in marinade for 4 hours, turning over every hour.

4.   When ready to smoke the chicken, supply your smoker with wood pellets and follow the manufacturer's specific start-up procedure. Preheat, with the lid closed, to 250ºF (121ºC).

5.   Remove the chicken from the marinade but do not rinse. Discard the marinade.

6.   Arrange the chicken directly on the grill, close the lid, and smoke for 1 hour 30 minute to 2 hours, or until a meat thermometer inserted in the thickest part of the meat reads 165ºF (74ºC).

7.   Let the meat rest for 3 minutes before serving.

CHAPTER 7 SEAFOOD

Pacific Northwest Salmon Fillet

Prep time: 15 minutes | Cook time: 1¼ hours | Serves 4

1 (2-pound / 907-g) half salmon fillet

1 batch dill seafood rub

2 tablespoons butter, cut into 3 or 4 slices

1.   Supply your smoker with wood pellets and follow the manufacturer's specific start-up procedure. Preheat the grill, with the lid closed, to 180ºF (82ºC).

2.   Season the salmon all over with the rub. Using your hands, work the rub into the flesh.

3.   Place the salmon directly on the grill grate, skin-side down, and smoke for 1 hour.

4.   Place the butter slices on the salmon, equally spaced. Increase the grill's temperature to 300ºF (149ºC) and continue to cook until the salmon's internal temperature reaches 145°F (63ºC). Remove the salmon from the grill and serve immediately.

Grilled Salmon Fillet

Prep time: 25 minutes | Cook time: 25 minutes | Serves 4

1 (2-pound / 907-g) half salmon fillet

3 tablespoons mayonnaise

1 batch dill seafood rub

1.   Supply your smoker with wood pellets and follow the manufacturer's specific start-up procedure. Preheat the grill, with the lid closed, to 325ºF (163ºC).

2.   Using your hands, rub the salmon fillet all over with the mayonnaise and sprinkle it with the rub.

3.   Place the salmon directly on the grill grate, skin-side down, and grill until its internal temperature reaches 145°F (63ºC). Remove the salmon from the grill and serve immediately.

Hot-Smoked Salmon Fillet

Prep time: 15 minutes | Cook time: 4 to 6 hours | Serves 4

1 (2-pound / 907-g) half salmon fillet

1 batch dill seafood rub

1.   Supply your smoker with wood pellets and follow the manufacturer's specific start-up procedure. Preheat the grill, with the lid closed, to 180°F (82°C).

2.   Season the salmon all over with the rub. Using your hands, work the rub into the flesh.

3.   Place the salmon directly on the grill grate, skin-side down, and smoke until its internal temperature reaches 145°F (63°C). Remove the salmon from the grill and serve immediately.

Wood-Fired Halibut Fillet

Prep time: 5 minutes | Cook time: 20 minutes | Serves 4

1 pound (454 g) halibut fillet

1 batch dill seafood rub

1.   Supply your smoker with wood pellets and follow the manufacturer's specific start-up procedure. Preheat the grill, with the lid closed, to 325°F (163°C).

2.   Sprinkle the halibut fillet on all sides with the rub. Using your hands, work the rub into the meat.

3.   Place the halibut directly on the grill grate and grill until its internal temperature reaches 145°F (63°C). Remove the halibut from the grill and serve immediately.

Grilled Tuna Steaks

Prep time: 10 minutes | Cook time: 10 minutes | Serves 2

2 (1½- to 2-inch-thick) tuna steaks

2 tablespoons olive oil

Salt, to taste

Freshly ground black pepper, to taste

1.   Supply your smoker with wood pellets and follow the manufacturer's specific start-up procedure. Preheat the grill, with the lid closed, to 500°F (260°C).

2.   Rub the tuna steaks all over with olive oil and season both sides with salt and pepper.

3.   Place the tuna steaks directly on the grill grate and grill for 3 to 5 minutes per side, leaving a pink center. Remove the tuna steaks from the grill and serve immediately.

BBQ Shrimp

Prep time: 15 minutes | Cook time: 10 minutes | Serves 4

1 pound (454 g) peeled and deveined shrimp, with tails on

2 tablespoons olive oil

1 batch dill seafood rub

1. Soak wooden skewers in water for 30 minutes.

2. Supply your smoker with wood pellets and follow the manufacturer's specific start-up procedure. Preheat the grill, with the lid closed, to 375°F (191°C).

3. Thread 4 or 5 shrimp per skewer.

4. Coat the shrimp all over with olive oil and season each side of the skewers with the rub.

5. Place the skewers directly on the grill grate and grill the shrimp for 5 minutes per side. Remove the skewers from the grill and serve immediately.

Buttered Cajun Shrimp

Prep time: 10 minutes | Cook time: 20 minutes | Serves 4

1 pound (454 g) peeled and deveined shrimp, with tails on

1 batch Cajun rub

8 tablespoons (1 stick) butter

¼ cup Worcestershire sauce

1. Supply your smoker with wood pellets and follow the manufacturer's specific start-up procedure. Preheat the grill, with the lid closed, to 450°F (232°C) and place a cast-iron skillet on the grill grate. Wait about 10 minutes after your grill has reached temperature, allowing the skillet to get hot.

2. Meanwhile, season the shrimp all over with the rub.

3. When the skillet is hot, place the butter in it to melt. Once the butter melts, stir in the Worcestershire sauce.

4. Add the shrimp and gently stir to coat. Smoke-braise the shrimp for about 10 minutes per side, until opaque and cooked through. Remove the shrimp from the grill and serve immediately.

Lemon Buttered Oysters

Prep time: 5 minutes | Cook time: 20 minutes | Serves 4

8 medium oysters, unopened, in the shell, rinsed and scrubbed

1 batch lemon butter mop for seafood

1. Supply your smoker with wood pellets and follow the manufacturer's specific start-up procedure. Preheat the grill, with the lid closed, to 375°F (191°C).

2. Place the unopened oysters directly on the grill grate and grill for about 20 minutes, or until the oysters are done and their shells open.

3. Discard any oysters that do not open. Shuck the remaining oysters, transfer them to a bowl, and add the mop. Serve immediately.

Cajun Catfish Fillet

Prep time: 15 minutes | Cook time: 15 minutes | Serves 6

2½ pounds catfish fillets

2 tablespoons olive oil

1 batch Cajun Rub

1. Supply your smoker with wood pellets and follow the manufacturer's specific start-up procedure. Preheat the grill, with the lid closed, to 300°F (149°C).

2. Coat the catfish fillets all over with olive oil and season with the rub. Using your hands, work the rub into the flesh.

3. Place the fillets directly on the grill grate and smoke until their internal temperature reaches 145°F (63°C). Remove the catfish from the grill and serve immediately.

King Crab Legs

Prep time: 5 minutes | Cook time: 10 minutes | Serves 4

8 King crab legs

A dipping sauce of your choice

1. Supply your smoker with wood pellets and follow the manufacturer's specific start-up procedure. Preheat the grill, with the lid closed, to 325°F (163°C).

2. Place the crab legs directly on the grill grate and grill for 10 minutes, flipping once after 5 minutes. Serve the crab with the mop on the side for dipping.

Grilled Lobster Tail

Prep time: 25 minutes | Cook time: 25 minutes | Serves 2

2 lobster tails

Salt, to taste

Freshly ground black pepper, to taste

1 batch lemon butter mop for seafood

1.   Supply your smoker with wood pellets and follow the manufacturer's specific start-up procedure. Preheat the grill, with the lid closed, to 375°F (191ºC).

2.   Using kitchen shears, slit the top of the lobster shells, through the center, nearly to the tail. Once cut, expose as much meat as you can through the cut shell.

3.   Season the lobster tails all over with salt and pepper.

4.   Place the tails directly on the grill grate and grill until their internal temperature reaches 145°F (63ºC). Remove the lobster from the grill and serve with the mop on the side for dipping.

BBQ Scallops

Prep time: 10 minutes | Cook time: 10 minutes | Serves 4

1 pound (454 g) large scallops

2 tablespoons olive oil

1 batch dill seafood rub

1.   Supply your smoker with wood pellets and follow the manufacturer's specific start-up procedure. Preheat the grill, with the lid closed, to 375°F (191ºC).

2.   Coat the scallops all over with olive oil and season all sides with the rub.

3.   Place the scallops directly on the grill grate and grill for 5 minutes per side. Remove the scallops from the grill and serve immediately.

Charleston Crab Cakes

1¼ cups mayonnaise

¼ cup yellow mustard

2 tablespoons sweet pickle relish, with its juices

1 tablespoon smoked paprika

2 teaspoons Cajun seasoning

2 teaspoons prepared horseradish

1 teaspoon hot sauce

1 garlic clove, finely minced

2 pounds (907 g) fresh lump crabmeat, picked clean

20 butter crackers (such as Ritz brand), crushed

2 tablespoons Dijon mustard

1 cup mayonnaise

2 tablespoons freshly squeezed lemon juice

1 tablespoon salted butter, melted

1 tablespoon Worcestershire sauce

1 tablespoon Old Bay seasoning

2 teaspoons chopped fresh parsley

1 teaspoon ground mustard

2 eggs, beaten

¼ cup extra-virgin olive oil, divided

For the Remoulade

1.   In a small bowl, combine the mayonnaise, mustard, pickle relish, paprika, Cajun seasoning, horseradish, hot sauce, and garlic.

2.   Refrigerate until ready to serve.

For the Crab Cakes

1.   Supply your smoker with wood pellets and follow the manufacturer's specific start-up procedure. Preheat, with the lid closed, to 375°F (191ºC).

2.   Spread the crabmeat on a foil-lined baking sheet and place over indirect heat on the grill, with the lid closed, for 30 minutes.

3.   Remove from the heat and let cool for 15 minutes.

4.   While the crab cools, combine the crushed crackers, Dijon mustard, mayonnaise, lemon juice, melted butter, Worcestershire sauce, Old Bay, parsley, ground mustard, and eggs until well incorporated.

5.   Fold in the smoked crabmeat, then shape the mixture into 8 (1-inch-thick) crab cakes.

6.   In a large skillet or cast-iron pan on the grill, heat 2 tablespoons of olive oil. Add half of the crab cakes, close the lid, and smoke for 4 to 5 minutes on each side, or until crispy and golden brown.

7.   Remove the crab cakes from the pan and transfer to a wire rack to drain. Pat them to remove any excess oil.

8.   Repeat steps 6 and 7 with the remaining oil and crab cakes.

9.   Serve the crab cakes with the remoulade.

Tangy Rainbow Trout

Prep time: 10 minutes | Cook time: 1 to 2 hours | Serves 6

6 to 8 skin-on rainbow trout, cleaned and scaled

1 gallon orange juice

½ cup packed light brown sugar

¼ cup salt

1 tablespoon freshly ground black pepper

Nonstick spray, oil, or butter, for greasing

1 tablespoon chopped fresh parsley

1 lemon, sliced

1. Fillet the fish and pat dry with paper towels.

2. Pour the orange juice into a large container with a lid and stir in the brown sugar, salt, and pepper.

3. Place the trout in the brine, cover, and refrigerate for 1 hour.

4. Cover the grill grate with heavy-duty aluminum foil. Poke holes in the foil and spray with cooking spray (see Tip).

5. Supply your smoker with wood pellets and follow the manufacturer's specific start-up procedure. Preheat, with the lid closed, to 225°F (107°C).

6. Remove the trout from the brine and pat dry. Arrange the fish on the foil-covered grill grate, close the lid, and smoke for 1 hour 30 minutes to 2 hours, or until flaky.

7. Remove the fish from the heat. Serve garnished with the fresh parsley and lemon slices.

Dijon-Smoked Halibut Steak

Prep time: 25 minutes | Cook time: 2 hours | Serves 6

4 (6-ounce / 170-g) halibut steaks

¼ cup extra-virgin olive oil

2 teaspoons kosher salt

1 teaspoon freshly ground black pepper

½ cup mayonnaise

½ cup sweet pickle relish

¼ cup finely chopped sweet onion

¼ cup chopped roasted red pepper

¼ cup finely chopped tomato

¼ cup finely chopped cucumber

2 tablespoons Dijon mustard

1 teaspoon minced garlic

1.   Rub the halibut steaks with the olive oil and season on both sides with the salt and pepper. Transfer to a plate, cover with plastic wrap, and refrigerate for 4 hours.

2.   Supply your smoker with wood pellets and follow the manufacturer's specific start-up procedure. Preheat, with the lid closed, to 200°F (93°C).

3.   Remove the halibut from the refrigerator and rub with the mayonnaise.

4.   Put the fish directly on the grill grate, close the lid, and smoke for 2 hours, or until opaque and an instant-read thermometer inserted in the fish reads 140°F (60°C).

5.   While the fish is smoking, combine the pickle relish, onion, roasted red pepper, tomato, cucumber, Dijon mustard, and garlic in a medium bowl. Refrigerate the mustard relish until ready to serve.

Salmon with Avocado

Prep time: 20 minutes | Cook time: 6 hours | Serves 6

¼ cup salt

¼ cup sugar

1 tablespoon freshly ground black pepper

1 bunch dill, chopped

1 pound sashimi-grade salmon, skin removed

1 avocado, sliced

8 bagels

4 ounces (113 g) cream cheese

1 bunch alfalfa sprouts

1 (3.5-ounce / 99-g) jar capers

1. In a small bowl, combine the salt, sugar, pepper, and fresh dill to make the curing mixture. Set aside.
2. On a smooth surface, lay out a large piece of plastic wrap and spread half of the curing salt mixture in the middle, spreading it out to about the size of the salmon.
3. Place the salmon on top of the curing salt.
4. Top the fish with the remaining curing salt, covering it completely. Wrap the salmon, leaving the ends open to drain.
5. Place the wrapped fish in a rimmed baking pan or dish lined with paper towels to soak up liquid.
6. Place a weight on the salmon evenly, such as a pan with a couple of heavy jars of pickles on top.
7. Put the salmon pan with weights in the refrigerator. Place something (a dishtowel, for example) under the back of the pan in order to slightly tip it down so the liquid drains away from the fish.
8. Leave the salmon to cure in the refrigerator for 24 hours.
9. Place the wood pellets in the smoker, but do not follow the start-up procedure and do not preheat.
10. Remove the salmon from the refrigerator, unwrap it, rinse it off, and pat dry.
11. Put the salmon in the smoker while still cold from the refrigerator to slow down the cooking process. You'll need to use a cold-smoker attachment or enlist the help of a smoker tube to hold the temperature at 80°F and maintain that for 6 hours to absorb smoke and complete the cold-smoking process.
12. Remove the salmon from the smoker, place it in a sealed plastic bag, and refrigerate for 24 hours. The salmon will be translucent all the way through.
13. Thinly slice the lox and serve with sliced avocado, bagels, cream cheese, alfalfa sprouts, and capers.

Rizty Summer Paella

Prep time: 1 hour | Cook time: 45 minutes | Serves 6

6 tablespoons extra-virgin olive oil, divided, plus more for drizzling

2 green or red bell peppers, cored, seeded, and diced

2 medium onions, diced

2 garlic cloves, slivered

1 (29-ounce / 822-g) can tomato purée

1½ pounds chicken thighs

Kosher salt, to taste

1½ pounds (680 g) tail-on shrimp, peeled and deveined

1 cup dried thinly sliced chorizo sausage

1 tablespoon smoked paprika

1½ teaspoons saffron threads

2 quarts chicken broth

3½ cups white rice

2 (7½-ounce / 213-g) cans chipotle chiles in adobo sauce

1½ pounds (680 g) fresh clams, soaked in cold water for 15 to 20 minutes2 tablespoons chopped fresh parsley

2 lemons, cut into wedges, for serving

1. Make the sofrito: On the stove top, in a saucepan over medium-low heat, combine ¼ cup of olive oil, the bell peppers, onions, and garlic, and cook for 5 minutes, or until the onions are translucent.

2. Stir in the tomato purée, reduce the heat to low, and simmer, stirring frequently, until most of the liquid has evaporated, about 30 minutes. Set aside. (Note: The sofrito can be made in advance and refrigerated.)

3. Supply your smoker with wood pellets and follow the manufacturer's specific start-up procedure. Preheat, with the lid closed, to 450ºF (232ºC).

4. Heat a large paella pan on the smoker and add the remaining 2 tablespoons of olive oil.

5. Add the chicken thighs, season lightly with salt, and brown for 6 to 10 minutes, then push to the outer edge of the pan.

6. Add the shrimp, season with salt, close the lid, and smoke for 3 minutes.

7. Add the sofrito, chorizo, paprika, and saffron, and stir together.

8. In a separate bowl, combine the chicken broth, uncooked rice, and 1 tablespoon of salt, stirring until well combined.

9. Add the broth-rice mixture to the paella pan, spreading it evenly over the other ingredients.

10. Close the lid and smoke for 5 minutes, then add the chipotle chiles and clams on top of the rice.

11. Close the lid and continue to smoke the paella for about 30 minutes, or until all of the liquid is absorbed.

12. Remove the pan from the grill, cover tightly with aluminum foil, and let rest off the heat for 5 minutes.

13. Drizzle with olive oil, sprinkle with the fresh parsley, and serve with the lemon wedges.

Cheesy Potato

Prep time: 20 minutes | Cook time: 1½ hours | Serves 16

8 Idaho, Russet, or Yukon Gold potatoes

1 (12-ounce / 340-g) can evaporated milk, heated

1 cup (2 sticks) butter, melted

½ cup sour cream, at room temperature

1 cup grated Parmesan cheese

½ pound (227 g) bacon, cooked and crumbled

¼ cup chopped scallions

Salt, to taste

Freshly ground black pepper, to taste

1 cup shredded Cheddar cheese

1.   Supply your smoker with wood pellets and follow the manufacturer's specific start-up procedure. Preheat, with the lid closed, to 400ºF (204ºC).

2.   Poke the potatoes all over with a fork. Arrange them directly on the grill grate, close the lid, and smoke for 1 hour and 15 minutes, or until cooked through and they have some give when pinched.

3.   Let the potatoes cool for 10 minutes, then cut in half lengthwise.

4.   Into a medium bowl, scoop out the potato flesh, leaving ¼ inch in the shells; place the shells on a baking sheet.

5.   Using an electric mixer on medium speed, beat the potatoes, milk, butter, and sour cream until smooth.

6.   Stir in the Parmesan cheese, bacon, and scallions, and season with salt and pepper.

7.   Generously stuff each shell with the potato mixture and top with Cheddar cheese.

8.   Place the baking sheet on the grill grate, close the lid, and smoke for 20 minutes, or until the cheese is melted.

Cauliflower and Broccoli Salad

Prep time: 25 minutes | Cook time: 0 minute | Serves 4

1½ cups mayonnaise

½ cup sour cream

¼ cup sugar

1 bunch broccoli, cut into small pieces

1 head cauliflower, cut into small pieces

1 small red onion, chopped

6 slices bacon, cooked and crumbled (precooked bacon works well)

1 cup shredded Cheddar cheese

1. In a small bowl, whisk together the mayonnaise, sour cream, and sugar to make a dressing.
2. In a large bowl, combine the broccoli, cauliflower, onion, bacon, and Cheddar cheese.
3. Pour the dressing over the vegetable mixture and toss well to coat.
4. Serve the salad chilled.

BBQ Baked Beans

Prep time: 15 minutes | Cook time: 2 to 3 hours | Serves 12 to 15

3 (28-ounce / 794-g) cans baked beans

1 large onion, finely chopped

1 cup The Ultimate BBQ Sauce

½ cup light brown sugar

¼ cup Worcestershire sauce

3 tablespoons yellow mustard

Nonstick cooking spray or butter, for greasing

1 large bell pepper, cut into thin rings

½ pound thick-cut bacon, partially cooked and cut into quarters

1. Supply your smoker with wood pellets and follow the manufacturer's specific start-up procedure. Preheat, with the lid closed, to 300ºF (149ºC).
2. In a large mixing bowl, stir together the beans, onion, barbecue sauce, brown sugar, Worcestershire sauce, and mustard until well combined
3. Coat a 9-by-13-inch aluminum pan with cooking spray or butter.
4. Pour the beans into the pan and top with the bell pepper rings and bacon pieces, pressing them down slightly into the sauce.
5. Place a layer of heavy-duty foil on the grill grate to catch drips, and place the pan on top of the foil. Close the lid and cook for 2 hours 30 minutes to 3 hours, or until the beans are hot, thick, and bubbly.
6. Let the beans rest for 5 minutes before serving.

Homemade Blt Pasta Salad

Prep time: 10 minutes | Cook time: 35 to 45 minutes | Serves 6

1 pound (454 g) thick-cut bacon

16 ounces (454 g)bowtie pasta, cooked according to package directions and drained

2 tomatoes, chopped

½ cup chopped scallions

½ cup Italian dressing

½ cup ranch dressing

1 tablespoon chopped fresh basil

1 teaspoon salt

1 teaspoon freshly ground black pepper

1 teaspoon garlic powder

1 head lettuce, cored and torn

1.   Supply your smoker with wood pellets and follow the manufacturer's specific start-up procedure. Preheat, with the lid closed, to 225ºF (107ºC).

2.   Arrange the bacon slices on the grill grate, close the lid, and cook for 30 to 45 minutes, flipping after 20 minutes, until crisp.

3.   Remove the bacon from the grill and chop.

4.   In a large bowl, combine the chopped bacon with the cooked pasta, tomatoes, scallions, Italian dressing, ranch dressing, basil, salt, pepper, and garlic powder. Refrigerate until ready to serve.

5.   Toss in the lettuce just before serving to keep it from wilting.

CHAPTER 8 BURGERS

Smoked Beef Burgers

Prep time: 15 minutes | Cook time: 45 minutes | Serves 4

1 pound (454 g) ground beef

1 egg

Wood-Fired Burger Seasoning

1.   Supply your Traeger with wood pellets and follow the start-up procedure. Preheat the grill, with the lid closed, to 180°F (82°C).

2.   In a medium bowl, thoroughly mix together the ground beef and egg. Divide the meat into 4 portions and shape each into a patty. Season the patties with the burger shake.

3.   Place the burgers directly on the grill grate and smoke for 30 minute.

4.   Increase the grill's temperature to 400°F (204°C) and continue to cook the burgers until their internal temperature reaches 145°F (63°C). Remove the burgers from the grill and serve as you like.

Ranch Cheeseburgers

Prep time: 10 minute | Cook time: 30 minute | Serves 4

1 lb (454 g) ground beef (preferably 80% lean 20% fat ground chuck)

½ yellow onion, chopped

1(1-ounce / 28-g) package ranch dressing mix

1 cup cheddar cheese, shredded

1 egg, beaten

4 buns, toasted (optional)

¾ cup bread crumbs

¾ cup mayonnaise

¼cup relish

¼ cup ketchup

2 tablespoon Worcestershire sauce

1.   Mix ground beef, cheese, ranch dressing mix, egg, bread crumbs, and onion in a bowl until evenly combined.

2.   Form burger mixture into ¼ pound circular patties.

3.   Preheat pellet grill to 350°F (177°C).

4.   Lightly oil grill grate and place burger patties on the grill.

5.   Cook burgers until they reach an internal temperature of 155°F (68°C) (typically cooks for about 6 minutes per side).

6.   Remove burgers once done and let rest at room temperature for 15 minutes.

7.   Combine sauce ingredients in a bowl and whisk well.

8.   Place burger patties on buns and top with desired toppings, including homemade sauce.

Spicy Chunk Cheeseburgers

Prep time: 15 minutes | Cook time: 30 minute | Serves 4

1 lb (454 g) ground chuck (80% lean, 20% fat)

4 Monterey Jack cheese slices

¼ cup yellow onion, finely chopped

4 hamburger buns

2 tablespoon hatch chiles, peeled and chopped

6 tablespoon hatch chile salsa

1 teaspoon kosher salt

Mayonnaise, to taste

1 teaspoon ground black pepper

1.   In a bowl, combine beef, diced onion, chopped hatch chiles, salt, and fresh ground pepper. Once evenly mixed, shape into 4 burger patties

2.   Preheat pellet grill to 350ºF (177ºC)

3.   Place burgers on grill, and cook for about 6 minutes per side or until both sides of each burger are slightly crispy

4.   After burger is cooked to desired doneness and both sides have light sear, place cheese slices on each burger. Allow to heat for around 45 seconds or until cheese melts

5.   Remove from grill and allow to rest for about 10 minute6. Spread a little bit of mayonnaise on both sides of each bun. Place burger patty on bottom side of the bun, then top with hatch chile salsa on top to taste

Balsamic Mexican Street Corn

Prep time: 15 minutes | Cook time: 45 minutes | Serves 6

16 to 20 long toothpicks

1 pound (454 g) Brussels sprouts, trimmed and wilted, leaves removed

½ pound (227 g) bacon, cut in half

1 tablespoon packed brown sugar

1 tablespoon Cajun seasoning

¼ cup balsamic vinegar

¼ cup extra-virgin olive oil

¼ cup chopped fresh cilantro

2 teaspoons minced garlic

1.   Soak the toothpicks in water for 15 minutes.

2.   Supply your smoker with wood pellets and follow the manufacturer's specific start-up procedure. Preheat, with the lid closed, to 300ºF (149ºC).

3.   Wrap each Brussels sprout in a half slice of bacon and secure with a toothpick.

4.   In a small bowl, combine the brown sugar and Cajun seasoning. Dip each wrapped Brussels sprout in this sweet rub and roll around to coat.

5.   Place the sprouts on a Frogmat or parchment paper–lined baking sheet on the grill grate, close the lid, and smoke for 45 minutes to 1 hour, turning as needed, until cooked evenly and the bacon is crisp.

6.   In a small bowl, whisk together the balsamic vinegar, olive oil, cilantro, and garlic.

7.   Remove the toothpicks from the Brussels sprouts, transfer to a plate and serve drizzled with the cilantro-balsamic sauce.

Potato Fries with Chipotle Ketchup

Prep time: 10 minutes | Cook time: 10 to 15 minutes | Serves 4

Chipotle Ketchup:

4 whole chipotle peppers, chopped

1 cup ketchup

1 tablespoon extra-virgin olive oil

1 teaspoon garlic powder

1 teaspoon onion powder

1 tablespoon chili powder

1 tablespoon sugar

1 tablespoon cumin

1 whole limes

Fries:

6 whole Yukon gold potatoes, cut into thick strips

2 tablespoons butter, melted

1 tablespoon Traeger Beef Rub

¼ cup chopped flat-leaf parsley

1.   Stir together all the chipotle ketchup in a mixing bowl until combined. Place in the refrigerator for at least 1 hour to blend the flavors (making it one day ahead of time is even better if you can swing it).

2.   When ready to cook, set Traeger temperature to High and preheat, lid closed for 15 minutes.

3.   Place the potatoes in a bowl, drizzle with melted butter and sprinkle with the Beef rub, tossing to coat.

4.   Lay the potatoes on a Traeger Grilling Basket and bake for 10 to 15 minutes, or until the fries reach your desired level of crispiness

5.   Remove the fries from the grill to a serving bowl, and toss with parsley. Serve with the chipotle ketchup for dipping.

Romaine Salad with Bacon

Prep time: 5 minutes | Cook time: 20 minutes | Serves 2

Salad:

1 romaine lettuce heart, cut in half

1 teaspoon olive oil

Salt and freshly ground black pepper, to taste

2 teaspoons grated Parmesan cheese

6 slices cooked bacon, crumbled

Dressing:

¼ cup milk

2 teaspoons blue cheese

2 teaspoons mayonnaise

Salt and pepper, to taste

Garlic powder, to taste

1. When ready to cook, set Traeger temperature to 450ºF (232ºC) and preheat, lid closed for 15 minutes.

2. Drizzle the olive oil over both faces of the romaine. Season lettuce with salt, pepper, and Parmesan cheese.

3. Lay the romaine lettuce, face-down, on the grill and cook for 2 minutes.

4. Remove romaine from grill to a salad bowl. Make the dressing by mixing the blue cheese, mayonnaise, and milk in a small bowl. Season to taste with a little salt, pepper, and garlic powder.

5. Add the bacon to the salad bowl with romaine and pour over the dressing. Toss well and serve immediately.

Bacon-Wrapped Jalapeños

Prep time: 15 minutes | Cook time: 1 hour | Serves 4

12 medium jalapeño

8 ounces (227 g) cream cheese, softened

2 tablespoons Traeger Pork & Poultry Rub

1 cup grated cheese

6 slices bacon, cut in half

1. When ready to cook, set Traeger temperature to 180ºF (82ºC) and preheat, lid closed for 15 minutes. For optimal flavor, use Super Smoke if available.

2. Slice the jalapeños in half lengthwise. Scrape out any seeds and ribs with a small spoon or paring knife. In a bowl, stir together softened cream cheese with Traeger Pork & Poultry rub and grated cheese. Spoon the mixture into each jalapeño half. Wrap with bacon and secure with a toothpick.

3. Place the jalapeños on a rimmed baking sheet. Place on the grill and smoke for 30 minutes.

4. Increase the grill temperature to 375ºF (191ºC) and cook for an additional 30 minutes, or until bacon is cooked to desired doneness.

5. Serve warm.

Creamy Mashed Red Potatoes

Prep time: 15 minutes | Cook time: 40 minutes | Serves 4

8 large red potatoes

Salt and black pepper, to taste

½ cup heavy cream

¼ cup butter, softened

1.   When ready to cook, set temperature to 180ºF (82ºC) and preheat, lid closed for 15 minutes.

2.   Slice red potatoes in half lengthwise, then cut in half again to make quarters. Season potatoes with salt and pepper.

3.   Increase the heat to High and preheat. Once the grill is hot, place the potatoes directly on the grill. Every 15 minutes flip the potatoes to ensure all sides get color. Continue to do this until potatoes are fork-tender.

4.   When tender, mash potatoes with heavy cream, butter, salt, and pepper to taste. Serve immediately.

Herb-Infused Riced Potatoes

Prep time: 20 minutes | Cook time: 1 hour | Serves 6

2½ pounds (1.1 kg) russet potatoes, peeled and cut into 1-inch cubes

1½ cups water

1 cup heavy cream

6 sage leaves

3 thyme sprigs

2 rosemary sprigs

2 tablespoons thyme leaves

6 peppercorns

2 garlic cloves

2 butter, sticks

Salt and ground black pepper, to taste

1.   When ready to cook, set Traeger temperature to 350ºF (177ºC) and preheat, lid closed for 15 minutes.

2.   Place the potatoes in a heatproof dish with water, cover and cook for 1 hour or until fork-tender.

3.   Meanwhile, combine the heavy cream with the herbs, peppercorns, and garlic cloves in a small saucepan.

4.   Place on the grill, cover, and allow to steep for 15 minutes. Strain the cream through a sieve to remove the herbs and garlic, place back in the saucepan and keep warm on the stove.

5.   Drain and using a potato ricer, rice the potatoes back into the large stockpot. Slowly pour in two-thirds of the cream, then stir in 1 stick of the butter and 1 tablespoon of salt. Continue to add more cream, butter and salt to reach your desired consistency.

6.   Serve immediately.

Roasted Green Beans and Bacon

Prep time: 15 minutes | Cook time: 20 minutes | Serves 4

1½ pounds (680 g) fresh green beans

4 strips bacon, cut into small pieces

4 tablespoons extra-virgin olive oil

2 clove garlic, minced

1 teaspoon kosher salt

1.   When ready to cook, set Traeger temperature to High and preheat, lid closed for 15 minutes.

2.   Toss all ingredients together and spread out evenly on a sheet tray.

3.   Place the tray directly on the grill and roast until the bacon is crispy and beans are lightly browned, about 20 minutes. Serve hot.

Smoked Olives

Prep time: 10 minutes | Cook time: 20 to 30 minutes | Serves 4

1 pound (454 g) mixed olives

1 quart extra-virgin olive oil

1 whole lemon zest

1 whole orange zest

½ tablespoon red pepper flakes

½ tablespoon dried fennel seed

3 whole dried bay leaves

4 whole thyme sprigs

4 whole rosemary sprigs

1.   When ready to cook, set Traeger temperature to 225ºF (107ºC) and preheat, lid closed for 15 minutes. For optimal flavor, use Super Smoke if available.

2.   Spread the olives out on a roasting pan and place on the grill. Smoke for 20 to 30 minutes or until the olives have a smoky flavor.

3.   Remove from the grill when olives reach desired smokiness and cool. Once cooled, combine smoked olives, olive oil, orange and lemon zest, red pepper flakes, fennel, bay leaves, thyme, and rosemary. Store in an airtight container, ensuring all the olives are submerged. Serve.

CHAPTER 10 VEGETARIAN AND VEGAN

Mexican Street Corn

Prep time: 10 minutes | Cook time: 12 to 14 minutes | Serves 4

4 ears corn

½ cup sour cream

½ cup mayonnaise

1 cup grated Parmesan cheese

¼ cup chopped fresh cilantro, plus more for garnish

Chipotle Butter, for topping

1.   Supply your smoker with wood pellets and follow the manufacturer's specific start-up procedure. Preheat, with the lid closed, to 450ºF (232ºC).

2.   Shuck the corn, removing the silks and cutting off the cores.

3.   Tear four squares of aluminum foil large enough to completely cover an ear of corn.

4.   In a medium bowl, combine the sour cream, mayonnaise, and cilantro. Slather the mixture all over the ears of corn.

5.   Wrap each ear of corn in a piece of foil, sealing tightly. Place on the grill, close the lid, and smoke for 12 to 14 minutes.

6.   Remove the corn from the foil and place in a shallow baking dish. Top with chipotle butter, the Parmesan cheese, and more chopped cilantro.

7.   Serve immediately.

Smoked Okra

Prep time: 10 minutes | Cook time: 30 minutes | Serves 4

Nonstick cooking spray or butter, for greasing

1 pound (454 g) whole okra

2 tablespoons extra-virgin olive oil

2 teaspoons seasoned salt

2 teaspoons freshly ground black pepper

1.   Supply your smoker with wood pellets and follow the manufacturer's specific start-up procedure. Preheat, with the lid closed, to 400ºF (204ºC). Alternatively, preheat your oven to 400ºF (204ºC).

2.   Line a shallow rimmed baking pan with aluminum foil and coat with cooking spray.

3.   Arrange the okra on the pan in a single layer. Drizzle with the olive oil, turning to coat. Season on all sides with the salt and pepper.

4.   Place the baking pan on the grill grate, close the lid, and smoke for 30 minutes, or until crisp and slightly charred. Alternatively, roast in the oven for 30 minutes.

5.   Serve hot.

Garlic-Wine Buttered Spaghetti Squash

Prep time: 20 minutes | Cook time: 40 minutes | Serves 4

1 spaghetti squash

2 tablespoons extra-virgin olive oil

1 teaspoon salt

1 teaspoon freshly ground black pepper

2 teaspoons garlic powder

4 tablespoons (½ stick) unsalted butter

½ cup white wine

1 tablespoon minced garlic

2 teaspoons chopped fresh parsley

1 teaspoon red pepper flakes

½ teaspoon salt

½ teaspoon freshly ground black pepper

For the Squash

1. Supply your smoker with wood pellets and follow the manufacturer's specific start-up procedure. Preheat, with the lid closed, to 375°F (191ºC).

2. Cut off both ends of the squash, then cut it in half lengthwise. Scoop out and discard the seeds.

3. Rub the squash flesh well with the olive oil and sprinkle on the salt, pepper, and garlic powder.

4. Place the squash cut-side up on the grill grate, close the lid, and smoke for 40 minutes, or until tender

For the Sauce

1. On the stove top, in a medium saucepan over medium heat, combine the butter, white wine, minced garlic, parsley, red pepper flakes, salt, and pepper, and cook for about 5 minutes, or until heated through. Reduce the heat to low and keep the sauce warm.

2. Remove the squash from the grill and let cool slightly before shredding the flesh with a fork; discard the skin.

3. Stir the shredded squash into the garlic-wine butter sauce and serve immediately.

Georgia Parmesan Sweet Onion

Prep time: 25 minutes | Cook time: 1 hour | Serves 6

Nonstick cooking spray or butter, for greasing

4 large Vidalia or other sweet onions

8 tablespoons (1 stick) unsalted butter, melted

4 chicken bouillon cubes

1 cup grated Parmesan cheese

1.   Supply your smoker with wood pellets and follow the manufacturer's specific start-up procedure. Preheat, with the lid closed, to 350ºF (177ºC).

2.   Coat a high-sided baking pan with cooking spray or butter.

3.   Peel the onions and cut into quarters, separating into individual petals.

4.   Spread the onions out in the prepared pan and pour the melted butter over them.

5.   Crush the bouillon cubes and sprinkle over the buttery onion pieces, then top with the cheese.

6.   Transfer the pan to the grill, close the lid, and smoke for 30 minutes.

7.   Remove the pan from the grill, cover tightly with aluminum foil, and poke several holes all over to vent.

8.   Place the pan back on the grill, close the lid, and smoke for an additional 30 to 45 minutes.

9.   Uncover the onions, stir, and serve hot.

Crispy Sweet Potato Chips

Prep time: 40 minutes | Cook time: 35 to 45 minutes | Serves 3

2 sweet potatoes

1 quart warm water

1 tablespoon cornstarch, plus 2 teaspoons

¼ cup extra-virgin olive oil

1 tablespoon salt

1 tablespoon packed brown sugar

1 teaspoon ground cinnamon

1 teaspoon freshly ground black pepper

½ teaspoon cayenne pepper

1.   Using a mandolin, thinly slice the sweet potatoes.

2.   Pour the warm water into a large bowl and add 1 tablespoon of cornstarch and the potato slices. Let soak for 15 to 20 minutes.

3.   Supply your smoker with wood pellets and follow the manufacturer's specific start-up procedure. Preheat, with the lid closed, to 375°F (191ºC).

4.   Drain the potato slices, then arrange in a single layer on a perforated pizza pan or a baking sheet lined with aluminum foil. Brush the potato slices on both sides with the olive oil.

5.   In a small bowl, whisk together the salt, brown sugar, cinnamon, black pepper, cayenne pepper, and the remaining 2 teaspoons of cornstarch. Sprinkle this seasoning blend on both sides of the potatoes.

6.   Place the pan or baking sheet on the grill grate, close the lid, and smoke for 35 to 45 minutes, flipping after 20 minutes, until the chips curl up and become crispy.

7.   Store in an airtight container.

CHAPTER 11 APPETIZERS AND SNACKS

Smoked Salted Cashews

Prep time: 5 minutes | Cook time: 1 hour | Serves 6

1 pound (454 g) roasted, salted cashews

1.   Supply your smoker with wood pellets and follow the manufacturer's specific start-up procedure. Preheat the grill, with the lid closed, to 120ºF (49ºC).

2.   Pour the cashews onto a rimmed baking sheet and smoke for 1 hour, stirring once about halfway through the smoking time.

3.   Remove the cashews from the grill, let cool, and store in an airtight container for as long as you can resist.

Smoked Cheddar Cheese

Prep time: minutes | Cook time: 2½ hours | Serves 4

1 (2-pound / 907-g) block medium Cheddar cheese, or your favorite cheese, quartered lengthwise

1.   Supply your smoker with wood pellets and follow the manufacturer's specific start-up procedure. Preheat the grill, with the lid closed, to 90ºF (32ºC).

2.   Place the cheese directly on the grill grate and smoke for 2 hours, 30 minutes, checking frequently to be sure it's not melting. If the cheese begins to melt, try flipping it. If that doesn't help, remove it from the grill and refrigerate for about 1 hour and then return it to the cold smoker.

3.   Remove the cheese, place it in a zip-top bag, and refrigerate overnight.

4.   Slice the cheese and serve with crackers, or grate it and use for making a smoked mac and cheese.

Cheesy Bacon-Wrapped Jalapeño

Prep time: 20 minutes | Cook time: 30 minutes | Serves 12

8 ounces (227 g) cream cheese, softened

½ cup shredded Cheddar cheese

¼ cup chopped scallions

1 teaspoon chipotle chile powder or regular chili powder

1 teaspoon garlic powder

1 teaspoon salt

18 large jalapeño peppers, stemmed, seeded, and halved lengthwise

1 pound (454 g) bacon (precooked works well)

1.   Supply your smoker with wood pellets and follow the manufacturer's specific start-up procedure. Preheat, with the lid closed, to 350ºF (177ºC). Line a baking sheet with aluminum foil.

2.   In a small bowl, combine the cream cheese, Cheddar cheese, scallions, chipotle powder, garlic powder, and salt.

3.   Stuff the jalapeño halves with the cheese mixture.

4.   Cut the bacon into pieces big enough to wrap around the stuffed pepper halves.

5.   Wrap the bacon around the peppers and place on the prepared baking sheet.

6.   Put the baking sheet on the grill grate, close the lid, and smoke the peppers for 30 minutes, or until the cheese is melted and the bacon is cooked through and crisp.

7.   Let the jalapeño poppers cool for 3 to 5 minutes. Serve warm.

Pulled Pork Nachos with Avocado

Prep time: 15 minutes | Cook time: 10 minutes | Serves 4

2 cups leftover smoked pulled pork

1 small sweet onion, diced

1 medium tomato, diced

1 jalapeño pepper, seeded and diced

1 garlic clove, minced

1 teaspoon salt

1 teaspoon freshly ground black pepper

1 bag tortilla chips

1 cup shredded Cheddar cheese

½ cup The Ultimate BBQ Sauce, divided

½ cup shredded jalapeño Monterey Jack cheese

Juice of ½ lime

1 avocado, halved, pitted, and sliced

2 tablespoons sour cream

1 tablespoon chopped fresh cilantro

1.   Supply your smoker with wood pellets and follow the manufacturer's specific start-up procedure. Preheat, with the lid closed, to 375°F (191ºC).

2.   Heat the pulled pork in the microwave.

3.   In a medium bowl, combine the onion, tomato, jalapeño, garlic, salt, and pepper, and set aside.

4.   Arrange half of the tortilla chips in a large cast iron skillet. Spread half of the warmed pork on top and cover with the Cheddar cheese. Top with half of the onion-jalapeño mixture, then drizzle with ¼ cup of barbecue sauce.

5.   Layer on the remaining tortilla chips, then the remaining pork and the Monterey Jack cheese. Top with the remaining onion-jalapeño mixture and drizzle with the remaining ¼ cup of barbecue sauce.

6.   Place the skillet on the grill, close the lid, and smoke for about 10 minutes, or until the cheese is melted and bubbly. (Watch to make sure your chips don't burn!)

7.   Squeeze the lime juice over the nachos, top with the avocado slices and sour cream, and garnish with the cilantro before serving hot.

Pig Pops

Prep time: 15 minutes | Cook time: 25 to 30 minutes | Serves 24

Nonstick cooking spray, oil, or butter, for greasing

2 pounds (907 g) thick-cut bacon (24 slices)

24 metal skewers

1 cup packed light brown sugar

2 to 3 teaspoons cayenne pepper

½ cup maple syrup, divided

1.   Supply your smoker with wood pellets and follow the manufacturer's specific start-up procedure. Preheat, with the lid closed, to 350ºF (177ºC).

2.   Coat a disposable aluminum foil baking sheet with cooking spray, oil, or butter.

3.   Thread each bacon slice onto a metal skewer and place on the prepared baking sheet.

4.   In a medium bowl, stir together the brown sugar and cayenne.

5.   Baste the top sides of the bacon with ¼ cup of maple syrup.

6.   Sprinkle half of the brown sugar mixture over the bacon.

7.   Place the baking sheet on the grill, close the lid, and smoke for 15 to 30 minutes.

8.   Using tongs, flip the bacon skewers. Baste with the remaining ¼ cup of maple syrup and top with the remaining brown sugar mixture.

9.   Continue smoking with the lid closed for 10 to 15 minutes, or until crispy. You can eyeball the bacon and smoke to your desired doneness, but the actual ideal internal temperature for bacon is 155°F (68ºC).

10. Using tongs, carefully remove the bacon skewers from the grill. Let cool completely before handling.

Chorizo Queso Fundido with Tortilla Chips

Prep time: 40 minutes | Cook time: 20 minutes | Serves 4 to 6

1 poblano chile

1 cup chopped queso quesadilla or queso Oaxaca

1 cup shredded Monterey Jack cheese

¼ cup milk

1 tablespoon all-purpose flour

2 (4-ounce / 113-g) links Mexican chorizo sausage, casings removed

⅓ cup beer

1 tablespoon unsalted butter

1 small red onion, chopped

½ cup whole kernel corn

2 serrano chiles or jalapeño peppers, stemmed, seeded, and coarsely chopped

1 tablespoon minced garlic

1 tablespoon freshly squeezed lime juice

1 teaspoon ground cumin

1 teaspoon salt

1 teaspoon freshly ground black pepper

1 tablespoon chopped fresh cilantro

1 tablespoon chopped scallions

Tortilla chips, for serving

1.   Supply your smoker with wood pellets and follow the manufacturer's specific start-up procedure. Preheat, with the lid closed, to 350ºF (177ºC).

2.   On the smoker or over medium-high heat on the stove top, place the poblano directly on the grate (or burner) to char for 1 to 2 minutes, turning as needed. Remove from heat and place in a closed-up lunch-size paper bag for 2 minutes to sweat and further loosen the skin.

3.   Remove the skin and coarsely chop the poblano, removing the seeds; set aside.

4.   In a bowl, combine the queso quesadilla, Monterey Jack, milk, and flour; set aside.

5.   On the stove top, in a cast iron skillet over medium heat, cook and crumble the chorizo for about 2 minutes.

6.   Transfer the cooked chorizo to a small, grill-safe pan and place over indirect heat on the smoker.

7.   Place the cast iron skillet on the preheated grill grate. Pour in the beer and simmer for a few minutes, loosening and stirring in any remaining sausage bits from the pan.

8.   Add the butter to the pan, then add the cheese mixture a little at a time, stirring constantly.

9.   When the cheese is smooth, stir in the onion, corn, serrano chiles, garlic, lime juice, cuvmin, salt, and pepper. Stir in the reserved chopped charred poblano.

10. Close the lid and smoke for 15 to 20 minutes to infuse the queso with smoke flavor and further cook the vegetables.

11. When the cheese is bubbly, top with the chorizo mixture and garnish with the cilantro and scallions.

12. Serve the chorizo queso fundido hot with tortilla chips.

Cream Cheese Hot Sausage Balls

Prep time: 15 minutes | Cook time: 30 minutes | Serves 4 to 5

1 pound (454 g) ground hot sausage, uncooked

8 ounces (227 g) cream cheese, softened

1 package mini filo dough shells

1.   Supply your smoker with wood pellets and follow the manufacturer's specific start-up procedure. Preheat, with the lid closed, to 350ºF (177ºC).

2.   In a large bowl, using your hands, thoroughly mix together the sausage and cream cheese until well blended.

3.   Place the filo dough shells on a rimmed perforated pizza pan or into a mini muffin tin.

4.   Roll the sausage and cheese mixture into 1-inch balls and place into the filo shells.

5.   Place the pizza pan or mini muffin tin on the grill, close the lid, and smoke the sausage balls for 30 minutes, or until cooked through and the sausage is no longer pink.

6.   Plate and serve warm.

Dijon Pigs in a Blanket

Prep time: 20 minutes | Cook time: 15 minutes | Serves 4 to 6

2 tablespoon poppy seeds

1 tablespoon dried minced onion

2 teaspoon garlic, minced

2 tablespoon sesame seeds

1 teaspoon salt

8 ounce (227 g) original crescent dough

¼ cup Dijon mustard

1 large egg, beaten

1.   When ready to cook, start your Traeger at 350ºF (177ºC), and preheat with lid closed, 10 to 15 minutes.

2.   Mix together poppy seeds, dried minced onion, dried minced garlic, salt and sesame seeds. Set aside.

3.   Cut each triangle of crescent roll dough into thirds lengthwise, making 3 small strips from each roll.

4.   Brush the dough strips lightly with Dijon mustard. Put the mini hot dogs on 1 end of the dough and roll up.

5.   Arrange them, seam side down, on a greased baking pan. Brush with egg wash and sprinkle with seasoning mixture.

6.   Bake in Traeger until golden brown, about 12 to 15 minutes.

7.   Serve with mustard or dipping sauce of your choice. Enjoy!

Bacon Pork Pinwheels

Prep time: 10 minutes | Cook time: 20 minutes | Serves 4 to 6

1 whole pork loin, boneless

Salt and pepper, to taste

Greek seasoning, to taste

4 slices bacon

The ultimate BBQ sauce, to taste

1.   When ready to cook, start the Traeger and set temperature to 500ºF (260ºC). Preheat, lid closed, for 10 to 15 minutes.

2.   Trim pork loin of any unwanted silver skin or fat. Using a sharp knife, cut pork loin length wise, into 4 long strips.

3.   Lay pork flat, then season with salt, pepper and Cavender's Greek Seasoning.

4.   Flip the pork strips over and layer bacon on unseasoned side. Begin tightly rolling the pork strips, with bacon being rolled up on the inside.

5.   Secure a skewer all the way through each pork roll to secure it in place. Set the pork rolls down on grill and cook for 15 minutes.

6.   Brush BBQ Sauce over the pork. Turn each skewer over, then coat the other side. Let pork cook for another 5-10 minutes, depending on thickness of your pork. Enjoy!

Deviled Crab Appetizer

Prep time: 25 minutes | Cook time: 10 minutes | Makes 30 mini crab cakes

Nonstick cooking spray, oil, or butter, for greasing

1 cup panko breadcrumbs, divided

1 cup canned corn, drained

½ cup chopped scallions, divided

½ red bell pepper, finely chopped

16 ounces (454 g) jumbo lump crabmeat

¾ cup mayonnaise, divided

1 egg, beaten

1 teaspoon salt

1 teaspoon freshly ground black pepper

2 teaspoons cayenne pepper, divided

Juice of 1 lemon

1. Supply your smoker with wood pellets and follow the manufacturer's specific start-up procedure. Preheat, with the lid closed, to 425ºF (218ºC).
2. Spray three 12-cup mini muffin pans with cooking spray and divide ½ cup of the panko between 30 of the muffin cups, pressing into the bottoms and up the sides. (Work in batches, if necessary, depending on the number of pans you have.)
3. In a medium bowl, combine the corn, ¼ cup of scallions, the bell pepper, crabmeat, half of the mayonnaise, the egg, salt, pepper, and 1 teaspoon of cayenne pepper.
4. Gently fold in the remaining ½ cup of breadcrumbs and divide the mixture between the prepared mini muffin cups.
5. Place the pans on the grill grate, close the lid, and smoke for 10 minutes, or until golden brown.
6. In a small bowl, combine the lemon juice and the remaining mayonnaise, scallions, and cayenne pepper to make a sauce.
7. Brush the tops of the mini crab cakes with the sauce and serve hot.

Cheesy Smoked Turkey Sandwich

Prep time: 15 minutes | Cook time:15 minutes | Serves 1

2 slices sourdough bread

2 tablespoons butter, at room temperature

2 (1-ounce / 28-g) slices Swiss cheese

4 ounces (113 g) leftover smoked turkey

1 teaspoon garlic salt

1. Supply your smoker with wood pellets and follow the manufacturer's specific start-up procedure. Preheat the grill, with the lid closed, to 375˚F (191ºC).
2. Coat one side of each bread slice with 1 tablespoon of butter and sprinkle the buttered sides with garlic salt.
3. Place 1 slice of cheese on each unbuttered side of the bread, and then put the turkey on the cheese.
4. Close the sandwich, buttered sides out, and place it directly on the grill grate. Cook for 5 minutes. Flip the sandwich and cook for 5 minutes more. Remove the sandwich from the grill, cut it in half, and serve.

CHAPTER 12 DESSERTS

Bacon and Chocolate Cookies

Prep time: 20 minutes | Cook time: 10 to 12 minutes | Makes 2 douncesen cookies

2¾ cups all-purpose flour

1½ teaspoons baking soda

½ teaspoon salt

12 tablespoons (1½ sticks) unsalted butter, softened

1 cup light brown sugar

1 cup granulated sugar

2 eggs, at room temperature

2½ teaspoons apple cider vinegar

1 teaspoon vanilla extract

2 cups semisweet chocolate chips

8 slices bacon, cooked and crumbled

1.   In a large bowl, combine the flour, baking soda, and salt, and mix well.

2.   In a separate large bowl, using an electric mixer on medium speed, cream the butter and sugars. Reduce the speed to low and mix in the eggs, vinegar, and vanilla.

3.   With the mixer speed still on low, slowly incorporate the dry ingredients, chocolate chips, and bacon pieces.

4.   Supply your smoker with wood pellets and follow the manufacturer's specific start-up procedure. Preheat, with the lid closed, to 375°F (191ºC).

5.   Line a large baking sheet with parchment paper.

6.   Drop rounded teaspoonfuls of cookie batter onto the prepared baking sheet and place on the grill grate. Close the lid and smoke for 10 to 12 minutes, or until the cookies are browned around the edges.

Fast S'Mores Dip Skillet

Prep time: 5 minutes | Cook time: 6 to 8 minutes | Serves 4 to 6

2 tablespoons salted butter, melted

¼ cup milk

12 ounces (340 g) semisweet chocolate chips

16 ounces (454 g) Jet-Puffed marshmallows

Graham crackers and apple wedges, for serving

1.   Supply your smoker with wood pellets and follow the manufacturer's specific start-up procedure. Preheat, with the lid closed, to 450ºF (232ºC).

2.   Place a cast iron skillet on the preheated grill grate and pour in the melted butter and milk, stirring for about 1 minute.

3.   Once the mixture starts to heat, top with the chocolate chips in an even layer and arrange the marshmallows standing up to cover all of the chocolate.

4.   Close the lid and smoke for 5 to 7 minutes, or until the marshmallows are lightly toasted.

5.   Remove from the heat and serve immediately with graham crackers and apple wedges for dipping.

Blackberry Pie

Prep time: 15 minutes | Cook time: 20 to 25 minutes | Serves 4 to 6

Nonstick cooking spray or butter, for greasing

1 box (2 sheets) refrigerated piecrusts

8 tablespoons (1 stick) unsalted butter, melted, plus 8 tablespoons (1 stick) cut into pieces

½ cup all-purpose flour

2 cups sugar, divided

2 pints blackberries

½ cup milk

Vanilla ice cream, for serving

1.   Supply your smoker with wood pellets and follow the manufacturer's specific start-up procedure. Preheat, with the lid closed, to 375°F (191°C).

2.   Coat a cast iron skillet with cooking spray.

3.   Unroll 1 refrigerated piecrust and place in the bottom and up the side of the skillet. Using a fork, poke holes in the crust in several places.

4.   Set the skillet on the grill grate, close the lid, and smoke for 5 minutes, or until lightly browned. Remove from the grill and set aside.

5.   In a large bowl, combine the stick of melted butter with the flour and 1½ cups of sugar.

6.   Add the blackberries to the flour-sugar mixture and toss until well coated.

7.   Spread the berry mixture evenly in the skillet and sprinkle the milk on top. Scatter half of the cut pieces of butter randomly over the mixture.

8.   Unroll the remaining piecrust and place it over the top of skillet or slice the dough into even strips and weave it into a lattice. Scatter the remaining pieces of butter along the top of the crust.

9.   Sprinkle the remaining ½ cup of sugar on top of the crust and return the skillet to the smoker.

10. Close the lid and smoke for 15 to 20 minutes, or until bubbly and brown on top. It may be necessary to use some aluminum foil around the edges near the end of the cooking time to prevent the crust from burning.

11. Serve the pie hot with vanilla ice cream.

CHAPTER 13 BAKED GOODS

Egg White Glazed Pretzel Rolls

Prep time: 1 hour | Cook time: 20 minutes | Serves 6

2¾ cup bread flour

1 quick-rising yeast, envelope

1 teaspoon salt

1 teaspoon sugar

½ teaspoon celery seed

½ teaspoon caraway seeds

1 cup hot water

As needed cornmeal

8 cup water

¼ cup baking soda

2 tablespoon sugar

1 whole egg white

Coarse salt, to taste

1.   Combine bread flour, 1 envelope yeast, salt, 1 teaspoon sugar, caraway seeds and celery seeds in food processor or standing mixer with dough hook and blend.

2.   With machine running, gradually pour hot water, adding enough water to form smooth elastic dough. Process 1 minute to knead. (You could also knead it by hand for a few minutes.)

3.   Grease medium bowl. Add dough to bowl, turning to coat. Cover bowl with plastic wrap, then towel; let dough rise in warm draft-free area until doubled in volume, about 35 minutes.

4.   Flour a large baking sheet. Punch dough down and knead on lightly floured surface until smooth. Divide into 8 pieces. Form each dough piece into a ball.

5.   Place dough balls on prepared sheet, flattening each slightly. Using serrated knife, cut X in top center of each dough ball. Cover with towel and let dough balls rise until almost doubled in volume, about 20 minutes.

6.   When ready to cook, start the Traeger on Smoke with the lid open until a fire is established (4-5 minutes). Turn temperature to 375°F (191ºC) and preheat, lid closed, for 10 to 15 minutes.

7.   Grease another baking sheet and sprinkle with cornmeal. Bring water to boil in large saucepan. Add baking soda and sugar (water will foam up). Add 3 rolls (or however many will fit comfortably in the pot) and cook 30 seconds per side.

8.   Using slotted spoon, transfer rolls to prepared sheet, arranging X side up. Repeat with remaining rolls. Brush rolls with egg white glaze. Sprinkle rolls generously with coarse salt.

9.   Bake rolls until brown, about 20 to 25 minutes. Transfer to racks and cool 10 minutes. Serve rolls warm or at room temperature. Enjoy!

Italian Focaccia

Prep time: 25 minutes | Cook time: 40 minutes | Serves 6

1 cup warm water (110- to 115-ºF / 43- to 46-ºC)

½ ounce (14 g) yeast, active

1 teaspoon sugar

2½ cup flour

1 teaspoon salt

¼ cup extra-virgin olive oil

1½ teaspoon italian herbs, dried

⅛ teaspoon red pepper flakes

As needed coarse sea salt

1.   Measure the water in a glass-measuring cup. Stir in the yeast and sugar. Let rest for in a warm place. After 5 to 10 minutes, the mixture should be foamy, indicating the yeast is "alive." If it does not foam, discard it and start again.

2.   Pour the water/yeast mixture in the bowl of a food processor. Add 1 cup of the flour as well as the salt and ¼ cup of olive oil. Pulse several times to blend. Add the remaining flour, Italian herbs, and hot pepper flakes.

3.   Process the dough until it's smooth and elastic and pulls away from the sides of the bowl, adding small amounts of flour or water through the feed tube if the dough is respectively too wet or too dry.

4.   Let the dough rise in the covered food processor bowl in a warm place until doubled in bulk, about 1 hour.

5.   Remove the dough from the food processor (it will deflate) and turn onto a lightly floured surface.

6.   Oil two 8- to 9-inch round cake pans generously with olive oil. (Just pour a couple of glugs in and tilt the pan to spread the oil.) Divide the dough into two equal pieces, shape into disks, and put one in each prepared cake pan.

7.   Oil the top of each disk with olive oil and dimple the dough with your fingertips. Sprinkle lightly with coarse salt, and if desired, additional dried Italian herbs.

8.   Cover the focaccia dough with plastic wrap and let the dough rise in a warm place, about 45 minutes to an hour.

9.   When ready to cook, start the Traeger grill and set the temperature to 400F and preheat, lid closed, for 10 to 15 minutes.

10. Put the pans with the focaccia dough directly on the grill grate. Bake until the focaccia breads are light golden in color and baked through, 35 to 40 minutes, rotating the pans halfway through the baking time.

11. Let cool slightly before removing from the pans. Cut into wedges for serving.

Wheat Bread

Prep time: 30 minutes | Cook time: 1 hour | Serves 6

As needed extra-virgin olive oil

2 cup all-purpose flour

1 cup whole wheat flour

1¼ ounce (35 g) packet, active dry yeast

1¼ teaspoon salt

1½ cup water

As needed cornmeal

1.   Oil a large mixing bowl and set aside. In a second mixing bowl, combine the flours, yeast, and salt.

2.   Push your sleeve up to your elbow and form your fingers into a claw. Mix the dry ingredients until well-combined.

3.   Add the water and mix until blended. The dough will be wet, shaggy, and somewhat stringy.

4.   Tip the dough into the oiled mixing bowl and cover with plastic wrap.

5.   Allow the dough to rise at room temperature-- about 70ºF (21ºC)-- for 2 hours, or until the surface is bubbled.

6.   Turn the dough out onto a lightly floured work surface and lightly flour the top. With floured hands, fold the dough over on itself twice. Cover loosely with plastic wrap and allow the dough to rest for 15 minutes.

7.   Dust a clean lint-free cotton towel with cornmeal, wheat bran, or flour. With floured hands, gently form the dough into a ball and place it, seam side down, on the towel.

8.   Dust the top of the ball with cornmeal, wheat bran, or flour, and cover the dough with a second towel. Let the dough rise until doubled in size; the dough will not spring back when poked with a finger.

9.   In the meantime, start the Traeger grill and set temperature to 450ºF (232ºC). Preheat, lid closed, for 10-15 minutes.

10. Put a lidded 6- to 8-quart cast iron Dutch oven - preferably one coated with enamel, on the grill grate.

11. When the dough has risen, remove the top towel, slide your hand under the bottom towel to support the dough, then carefully tip the dough, seam side up, into the preheated pot.

12. Remove the towel. Shake the pot a couple of times if the dough looks lopsided: It will straighten out as it bakes.

13. Cover the pot with the lid and bake the bread for 30 minutes. Remove the lid and continue to bake the bread for 15 to 30 minutes more, or until it is nicely browned and sounds hollow when rapped with your knuckles.

14. Turn onto a wire rack to cool. Slice with a serrated knife. Enjoy!

Pepperoni Pizza Bites

Prep time: 1 day | Cook time: 20 minutes | Serves 6

4½ cup bread flour

1½ tablespoon sugar

2 teaspoon instant yeast

2 teaspoon kosher salt

3 tablespoon extra-virgin olive oil

15 fluid ounce (435 g) water, lukewarm

8 ounce (227 g)pepperoni, sliced

1 cup pizza sauce

1 cup Mounceszarella cheese

1 whole egg, for egg wash

As needed salt

1.   For the Pizza Dough: Combine flour, sugar, salt, and yeast in food processor. Pulse 3 to 4 times until incorporated evenly. Add olive oil and water. Run food processor until mixture forms ball that rides around the bowl above the blade, about 15 seconds. Continue processing 15 seconds longer.

2.   Transfer dough ball to lightly floured surface and knead once or twice by hand until smooth ball is formed. Divide dough into three even parts and place each into a 1 gallon zip top bag. Place in refrigerator and allow to rise at least one day.

3.   At least two hours before baking, remove dough from refrigerator and shape into balls by gathering dough towards bottom and pinching shut. Flour well and place each one in a separate medium mixing bowl. Cover tightly with plastic wrap and allow to rise at warm room temperature until roughly doubled in volume.

4.   When ready to cook, set the grill temperature to 350ºF (177ºC) and preheat, lid closed for 15 minutes.

5.   After the first rise remove the dough from the fridge and let come to room temperature. Roll dough on a flat surface. Cut dough into long strips 3" wide by 18" long.

6.   Slice pepperoni into strips.

7.   In a medium bowl combine the pizza sauce, mounceszarella and pepperoni.

8.   Spoon 1 tablespoon of the pizza filling onto the pizza dough every two inches, about halfway down the length of the dough. Dip a pastry brush into the egg wash and brush around pizza filling. Fold the half side of the dough (without the pizza filling) over the other the half that contains the pizza filling.

9.   Press down between each pizza bite slightly with your fingers. With a ravioli or pizza cutter, cut around each filling- creating a rectangle shape and sealing the crust in.

10. Transfer each pizza bite onto a parchment lined cookie sheet. Cover with a kitchen towel and let them rise for 30 minutes.

11. When ready to cook, preheat the grill to 350ºF (177ºC) with the lid closed for 10 to15 minutes.

12. Brush the bites with remaining egg wash, sprinkle with salt and place directly on the sheet tray. Bake 10 to 15 minutes until the exterior is golden brown.

13. Remove from grill and transfer to a serving dish. Serve with extra pizza sauce for dipping and enjoy!

Irish Bread

Prep time: 15 minutes | Cook time: 45 minutes | Serves 8 to 12

As needed cornmeal

3½ cup all-purpose flour

1½ teaspoon sugar

1¼ teaspoon baking soda

1 teaspoon salt

1 cup buttermilk

Butter, to taste

1. When ready to cook, set the temperature to 400ºF (204ºC) and preheat, lid closed, for 10 to 15 minutes.
2. Lightly dust the bottom of an 8-inch round cake pan with cornmeal and set aside.
3. Tear off a large sheet of wax paper and lay it on your work surface.
4. Combine the flour, sugar, soda, and salt in a large sifter and sift onto the wax paper. Carefully lift up the sides of the wax paper and tip the flour mixture back into the sifter. Re-sift into a large mixing bowl.
5. Lightly flour your work surface. Make a well in the middle of the flour mixture in the bowl and pour in 1 cup (240 mL) of buttermilk. Stir with a wooden spoon. Work quickly and gently as the carbon dioxide bubbles formed when the buttermilk hits the dry ingredients will deflate, the dough will look somewhat shaggy. If the dough seems dryish, add a little more buttermilk.
6. Turn out onto the floured surface, and with floured hands, knead gently for 10 to 20 seconds - just long enough to bring the dough bits together. (It will look more like biscuit dough than bread dough.)
7. Form into a flattish round and transfer to the prepared pan. Flour a sharp knife, and deeply cut a cross in the top of the loaf all the way to the edge of the bread. Quickly get it in to bake, if it sits too long, it will deflate.
8. Bake the bread for 45 to 50 minutes, or until it is browned and the bottom of the loaf sounds hollow when rapped with your knuckles.
9. Remove the bread from the baking pan and cool on a cooling rack. Just be-fore serving, cut the loaf in half and then slice each half into thin slices.
10. Serve with butter. Wrap leftovers tightly in plastic wrap or foil. This bread makes great toast. Enjoy!

Dinner Rolls

Prep time: 1 day | Cook time: 20 minutes | Serves 6

1 cup water, lukewarm

2 tablespoon yeast, quick rise

1 teaspoon salt

¼ cup sugar

3⅓ cup flour

¼ cup unsalted butter, softened

1 egg

As needed cooking spray

1 egg, for egg wash

1.   For the Pizza Dough: Combine flour, sugar, salt, and yeast in food processor. Pulse 3 to 4 times until incorporated evenly. Add olive oil and water. Run food processor until mixture forms ball that rides around the bowl above the blade, about 15 seconds. Continue processing 15 seconds longer.

2.   Transfer dough ball to lightly floured surface and knead once or twice by hand until smooth ball is formed. Divide dough into three even parts and place each into a 1 gallon zip top bag. Place in refrigerator and allow to rise at least one day.

3.   At least two hours before baking, remove dough from refrigerator and shape into balls by gathering dough towards bottom and pinching shut. Flour well and place each one in a separate medium mixing bowl. Cover tightly with plastic wrap and allow to rise at warm room temperature until roughly doubled in volume.

4.   When ready to cook, set the grill temperature to 350ºF (177ºC) and preheat, lid closed for 15 minutes.

5.   After the first rise remove the dough from the fridge and let come to room temperature. Roll dough on a flat surface. Cut dough into long strips 3" wide by 18" long.

6.   Slice pepperoni into strips.

7.   In a medium bowl combine the pizza sauce, mounceszarella and pepperoni.

8.   Spoon 1 tablespoon of the pizza filling onto the pizza dough every two inches, about halfway down the length of the dough. Dip a pastry brush into the egg wash and brush around pizza filling. Fold the half side of the dough (without the pizza filling) over the other the half that contains the pizza filling.

9.   Press down between each pizza bite slightly with your fingers. With a ravioli or pizza cutter, cut around each filling- creating a rectangle shape and sealing the crust in.

10. Transfer each pizza bite onto a parchment lined cookie sheet. Cover with a kitchen towel and let them rise for 30 minutes.

11. When ready to cook, preheat the grill to 350ºF (177ºC) with the lid closed for 10-15 minutes.

12. Brush the bites with remaining egg wash, sprinkle with salt and place directly on the sheet tray. Bake 10-15 minutes until the exterior is golden brown.

13. Remove from grill and transfer to a serving dish. Serve with extra pizza sauce for dipping and enjoy!

Rizty Pizza

Prep time: 20 minutes | Cook time: 12 minutes | Serves 6

⅔ cup warm water (10- to 115-ºF / 43- to 46-ºC)

2½ teaspoon active dry yeast

½ teaspoon granulated sugar

1 teaspoon kosher salt

1 tablespoon oil

2 cup all-purpose flour

¼ cup fine cornmeal

1 large grilled Portobello mushroom, sliced

1 jar pickled artichoke hearts, drained and chopped

1 cup shredded fontina cheese

½ cup shaved Parmigiano-Reggiano cheese, divided

To taste roasted garlic, minced

¼ cup extra-virgin olive oil

To taste banana peppers

1.   In a glass bowl, stir together the warm water, yeast and sugar. Let stand until the mixture starts to foam, about 10 minutes. In a mixer, combine 1¾ cup flour, sugar and salt. Stir oil into the yeast mixture. Slowly add the liquid to the dry ingredients while slowly increasing the mixers speed until fully combined. The dough should be smooth and not sticky.

2.   Knead the dough on a floured surface, gradually adding the remaining flour as needed to prevent the dough from sticking, until smooth, about 5 to 10 minutes.

3.   Form the dough into a ball. Apply a thin layer of olive oil to a large bowl. Place the dough into the bowl and coat the dough ball with a small amount of olive oil. Cover and let rise in a warm place for about 1 hour or until doubled in size.

4.   When ready to cook, set Traeger temperature to 450ºF (232ºC) and preheat, lid closed for 15 minutes.

5.   Place a pizza stone in the grill while it preheats.

6.   Punch the dough down and roll it out into a 12-inch circle on a floured surface.

7.   Spread the cornmeal evenly on the pizza peel. Place the dough on the pizza peel and assemble the toppings evenly in the following order: olive oil, roasted garlic, fontina, portobello, artichoke hearts, Parmigiano-Reggiano and banana peppers.

8.   Carefully slide the assembled pizza from the pizza peel to the preheated pizza stone and bake until the crust is golden brown, about 10 to 12 minutes. Enjoy!

Baked Pumpkin Bread

Prep time: 15 minutes | Cook time: 1 hour | Serves 6

1 cup pumpkin, canned

2 eggs

⅔ cup vegetable oil

½ cup sour cream

1 teaspoon vanilla extract

2½ cup flour

1½ teaspoon baking soda

1 teaspoon salt

½ teaspoon ground cinnamon

¼ teaspoon ground nutmeg

¼ teaspoon ground cloves

¼ teaspoon ground ginger

As needed butter

1.   In a large mixing bowl, combine the pumpkin, eggs, vegetable oil, sour cream, and vanilla and whisk to blend.

2.   In a separate bowl, combine the flour, baking soda, salt, cinnamon, nutmeg, cloves, and ginger. Add the dry ingredients to the wet ingredients and stir to combine. Do not overmix.

3.   If desired, stir in one or more of the optional ingredients (walnuts, dried cranberries, raisins, or chocolate chips). Butter the interiors of two loaf pans.

4.   Sprinkle with flour to coat the buttered surfaces, and tap out any excess. Divide the batter evenly between the two pans.

5.   When ready to cook, set the Traeger to 350ºF (177ºC) and preheat, lid closed for 15 minutes.

6.   Arrange the loaf pans directly on the grill grate. Bake for 45 to 50 minutes, or until a skewer or toothpick inserted in the center comes out clean. Also, the top of the loaf should spring back when pressed gently with a finger.

7.   Transfer the loaf pans to a cooling rack and let cool for 10 minutes before carefully turning out the pumpkin bread. Let the loaves cool thoroughly before slicing. Wrap in aluminum foil or plastic wrap if not eating right away. Serve and enjoy!